Better Homes and Gardens®

Christmas
1988

Time for Christmas

Christmas is a time of anticipation,
When hope becomes a shining star,
When children's wishes become prayers,
And days are X'ed on calendar.

Christmas is a time for healing,
When disagreers and disagreements meet,
When long-time wounds are mended
And love moves hatred to retreat.

Christmas is a time for patience,
When we try anew to mold
Our lives in the image of Him
Whose birthday we uphold.

Christmas is a time for giving,
The Wise Men brought their best,
But Christ showed that the gift of self
Will out-give all the rest.

Christmas is a time for understanding
People and customs throughout the world,
When for all-too-brief a season,
The banner of peace is unfurled.

Christmas is a time for sharing,
A time for needy hands to clasp,
A time for stretching out in faith
With a reach that exceeds our grasp.

Christmas is a time for children
No matter what their age,
Spirit is the only ticket,
And heart the only gauge.

Christmas is a time for love,
A time for inhibitions to shed,
A time for showing that we care,
A time for words too long unsaid.

Christmas is a time for learning,
A time when new truths unfold,
And not-so-innocent children
Often teach the old.

Christmas is a time to remember
Timeless stories from days of yore,
A time to ponder what's ahead,
A time to open another door.

—*Fred Bauer*

TABLE OF CONTENTS

A TIME FOR DREAMING

A TIME FOR REMEMBERING

A TIME FOR GIVING

Christmastime

A TIME FOR
DREAMING

Toyland

Toyland, Toyland,
Little girl and boy land,
While you dwell within it,
You are ever happy then.
Childhood's joyland,
Mystic, merry Toyland!
Once you pass its borders,
You can ne'er return again.

Jest 'fore Christmas

Father calls me William, sister calls me Will,
Mother calls me Willie, but the fellers call me Bill!
Mighty glad I ain't a girl—ruther be a boy,
Without them sashes, curls, an' things, that's worn by Fauntleroy!
Love to chawnk green apples an' go swimmin' in the lake—
Hate to take the castor-ile they give for belly-ache!
'Most all the time, the whole year round, there ain't no flies on me,
But jest 'fore Christmas I'm as good as I kin be!

Got a yeller dog named Sport, sick him on the cat;
First thing she knows she doesn't know where she is at!
Got a clipper sled, an' when us kids goes out to slide,
'Long comes the grocery cart, an' we all hook a ride!
But sometimes when the grocery man is worrited an' cross,
He reaches at us with his whip, an' larrups up his hoss,
An' then I laff an' holler, "Oh, ye never teched *me!*"
But jest 'fore Christmas I'm as good as I kin be!

Gran'ma says she hopes that when I git to be a man,
I'll be a missionarer like her oldest brother, Dan,
As was et up by the cannibuls that lives in Ceylon's Isle,
Where every prospeck pleases, an' only man is vile!
But gran'ma she has never been to see a Wild West show,
Nor read the Life of Daniel Boone, or else I guess she'd know
That Buff'lo Bill an' cow-boys is good enough for me!
Excep' jest 'fore Christmas, when I'm good as I kin be!

continued

And then old Sport he hangs around, so solemn-like an' still,
His eyes they seem a-sayin': "What's the matter, little Bill?"
The old cat sneaks down off her perch an' wonders what's become
Of them two enemies of hern that used to make things hum!
But I am so perlite an' 'tend so earnestly to biz,
That mother says to father: "How improved our Willie is!"
But father, havin' been a boy hisself, suspicions me
When, jest 'fore Christmas, I'm as good as I kin be!

For Christmas, with its lots an' lots of candies, cakes, an' toys,
Was made, they say, for proper kids, an' not for naughty boys:
So wash yer face an' bresh yer hair, an' mind yer p's and q's,
An' don't bust out yer pantaloons, and don't wear out yer shoes;
Say "Yessum" to the ladies, an' "Yessur" to the men,
An' when they's company, don't pass yer plate for pie again;
But, thinkin' of the things yer'd like to see upon that tree,
Jest 'fore Christmas be as good as yer kin be!

—Eugene Field

Sliding

We can slide
down the hill
or
down the stair

or
   down the street
      or anywhere.   Or
         down the roof
           where the shingles broke,   Or
                down the trunk
                  of the back-yard oak.
                Down the slide
                  or the ice
                    or the slippery street,

We can slide
   on our sled
      on our skates
         on our feet.

Oh, it's lots of fun to go outside
And slide
   and slide
      and slide
        and slide.

—Myra Cohn

Playtime characters step out of the storybooks and into the hearts of children, thanks to the delightful projects on the next few pages. With handcrafted touches of color and whimsy, the raggedy doll and clown shown here will come to life this Christmas morning.

Storybook Gifts For Children

Raggedy Doll And Clown Doll

Each doll is 21 inches tall.

MATERIALS
½ yard of 45-inch-wide
  unbleached muslin fabric
1 pound of polyester fiberfill
Pink, red, and black felt scraps
Dental floss
2 ounces of brown rug yarn
  (raggedy doll)
2 ounces of rust rug yarn
  (clown doll)
Fabric remnants of black (shoes),
  white (raggedy doll socks),
  red (clown arms), and
  pink/red stripe (raggedy
  doll legs)
⅔ yard of ½-inch-wide black
  satin ribbon (raggedy
  doll shoes)
⅔ yard of ½-inch-wide white
  lace (raggedy doll stockings)
Two small red pom-poms
  (clown shoes)
Tissue paper
Large darning needle (for
  sewing hair into dolls' heads)
Sewing threads to match doll
  body and each piece of
  doll clothing
Raggedy doll clothing
¼ yard of 45-inch-wide
  semisheer white fabric
  (panties, slip)
½ yard of 45-inch-wide pink/red
  print fabric (dress)
½ yard of ¼-inch-wide elastic

¾ yard of white rickrack (slip)
¾ yard of red double-fold
  bias tape
Two white ½-inch-diameter
  buttons
White fabric remnant (collar)
One 9x12-inch piece of red felt
1 yard of ⅜-inch-wide red satin
  ribbon (hat)
Clown clothing
Two ¼-yard pieces of
  coordinating green prints
  (trousers)
½ yard of green/white stripe
  fabric (shirt)
¼ yard of ¼-inch-wide elastic
¾ yard of green double-fold
  bias tape
Two small red pom-poms
¼ yard of red/black dot fabric
  (neck ruffle)
¾ yard of white piping
  (neck ruffle)
¾ yard of red double-fold
  bias tape
One 9x12-inch piece of red
  felt (hat)
One large white pom-pom (hat)

INSTRUCTIONS
Note: The same body pattern is
used for both of the dolls. The fabric yardages are based on 45-inch-
wide fabrics.

All patterns and measurements
include ¼-inch seam allowances
unless otherwise noted. Sew
seams and darts with right sides of
fabric facing. Clip curved seam allowances and press seams open
where possible.

Enlarge the doll patterns, *pages
18–21,* onto paper; cut out. Cut
the pieces from appropriate fabrics (see the materials list). In addition, cut and sew together the
following pieces before cutting
out the legs:

For raggedy-doll legs, cut one
3x19-inch piece of black fabric
(shoes), one 1¾x19-inch piece of
white fabric (stockings), and one
8x19-inch piece of pink/red stripe
(legs). Sew strips together, in order, along long edges; cut doll's
legs from pieced fabric, following
lines indicated on pattern.

For clown legs, cut one 3x19-inch
piece of black fabric (shoes) and
one 9½x19-inch piece from muslin. Sew the strips together along
the long edges; cut the clown's
legs from the pieced fabric.

BODY: Sew body front and
back darts; sew center back seam.
Sew chin to front, matching centers. Sew face to chin, matching
centers. Sew front to back, leaving
the bottom open for turning. Turn
right side out and stuff firmly; slip-
stitch the opening closed.

ARMS: Sew arm fronts and
backs together, leaving the tops
open. Turn arms right side out.
Stuff them firmly with fiberfill to
within an inch of the open ends.
Turn the raw edges in ¼ inch and
slip-stitch arms closed. Ladder-
stitch the arms to the upper body
continued

17

sides with dental floss, making sure thumbs are facing up.

LEGS: Assemble legs as for arms. Trim the shoes with bows or pom-poms; tack raggedy doll's lace to the tops of her stockings.

FACIAL DETAILS: *For raggedy doll,* cut eyes, cheeks, and nose from felt scraps; hand-sew to face. Accent eyes with French knots, using two strands of white floss. Outline-stitch the smile with three strands of red floss. Straight-stitch eyelashes with two strands of black floss. Tack mouth ovals atop the smile.

For clown, repeat as for raggedy doll except for nose. For the clown nose, butt the long straight nose edges together and whip-stitch closed. Gather ¼ inch from the curved edge, pulling the gathers slightly. Stuff nose. Slip-stitch the stuffed nose to the clown face.

HAIR: *For raggedy doll,* make each hair bunch by wrapping yarn around three of your fingers six times. Tie the bunch with yarn, then cut the ends opposite the tie. Tack to the doll's head. Continue making bunches of hair until you have enough to cover doll's head.

For clown, make each hair bunch by wrapping yarn around two of your fingers 10 times. Continue as for the raggedy doll. Trim the hair as needed.

Clothing

Enlarge the hat, collar, and yoke patterns, *pages 18–21,* onto paper. Cut the pattern pieces from the appropriate fabrics (see the materials list).

In addition, cut the following: *For the raggedy doll,* cut two 7½x11-inch pantie pieces and one 8x24-inch slip from the white semisheer fabric. For the dress pieces, cut

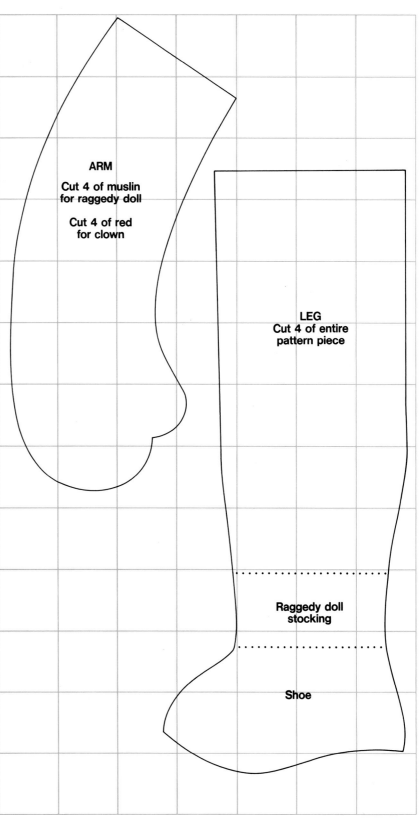

ARM

Cut 4 of muslin for raggedy doll

Cut 4 of red for clown

LEG

Cut 4 of entire pattern piece

Raggedy doll stocking

Shoe

1 Square = 1 Inch

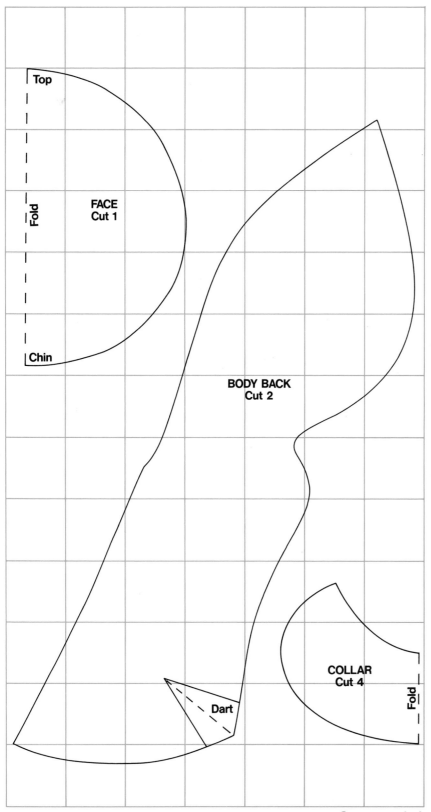

Top

Fold

FACE
Cut 1

Chin

BODY BACK
Cut 2

COLLAR
Cut 4

Fold

Dart

1 Square = 1 Inch

one 7½x13-inch dress front, two 7x7½-inch dress backs, and two 7½x9½-inch sleeves from the pink-and-red print.

For the clown doll, cut one 12½-inch square from each of the two green print fabrics (trousers).

For the clown doll's shirt, cut one 6½x13-inch shirt front, two 6½x7-inch shirt backs, and two 7½x9½-inch sleeves from green-and-white striped fabric. For neck ruffle, cut two 2½x24-inch strips from red-and-black dotted fabric.

PANTIES/TROUSERS: To hem, turn under ¼ inch twice on one long edge of each piece; stitch. Zigzag-stitch elastic 1 inch from the hems, pulling the elastic taut to gather the leg ruffle.

Sew the 5-inch-long center front and back seams. Turn under top edge and zigzag-stitch elastic along the inside edge, pulling the elastic taut to gather waist. Sew inner leg seams.

RAGGEDY-DOLL SLIP: Sew short sides together. For hem, turn under ¼ inch and sew. Trim hem with rickrack. Turn under top edge and zigzag-stitch elastic along the inside edge, pulling the elastic taut to gather the waist.

DRESS/SHIRT: Turn under the center back yoke edges ¼ inch. Bind neck edge of yoke with bias tape, extending the bias ends for back-of-the-neck ties.

Gather one long edge of the dress or shirt front, pulling the gathers to fit the yoke front edge; sew front to the yoke.

For the center backs, finish one edge of each back with a narrow hem. Gather the top edge of each dress or shirt back to fit the yoke back; sew dress or shirt to yoke back edges.

continued

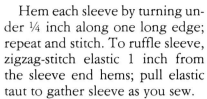

Hem each sleeve by turning under ¼ inch along one long edge; repeat and stitch. To ruffle sleeve, zigzag-stitch elastic 1 inch from the sleeve end hems; pull elastic taut to gather sleeve as you sew.

Gather center 6 inches of the sleeve tops, pulling up gathers to measure 2½ inches. Sew sleeve tops to yoke, matching centers. Sew underarm/side seams. Hem shirt or dress. Sew buttons or pom-poms to center front.

RAGGEDY-DOLL COLLAR: Sew the four collar pieces together in pairs, leaving openings for turning. Turn two collar sections right side out; sew openings closed. Tack collars together at front; put on doll and tack together at back.

CLOWN NECK RUFFLE: With raw edges even, baste piping to the right side of one long edge. With right sides facing, sew together the two ruffle strips at the short ends and along piped edge. Turn right side out. Gather along remaining raw edges, pulling up the gathers to fit the neck. Bind raw edges with red bias tape, extending the tape ends for ties.

RAGGEDY-DOLL HAT: Sew center back seam. With right sides facing and back seam at center, fold the hat following the dashed lines on the pattern. Sew across the solid line; trim away excess. Sew ribbon tie to the bottom edge of the hat between dots, extending ribbon ends equally for ties. Fold back hat brim and tie onto doll's head.

CLOWN HAT: Sew center back seam. Turn under curved edge ¼ inch and sew. Turn right side out and sew pom-pom to hat top. Tack to clown's head.

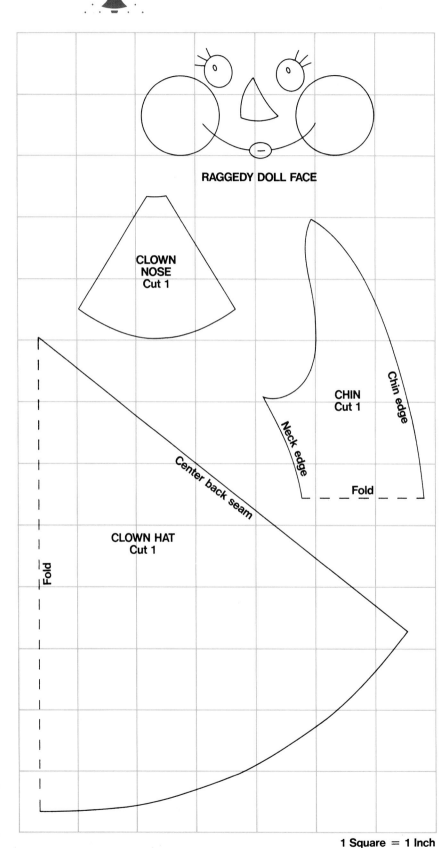

RAGGEDY DOLL FACE

CLOWN NOSE Cut 1

CHIN Cut 1

Chin edge

Neck edge

Fold

Center back seam

CLOWN HAT Cut 1

Fold

1 Square = 1 Inch

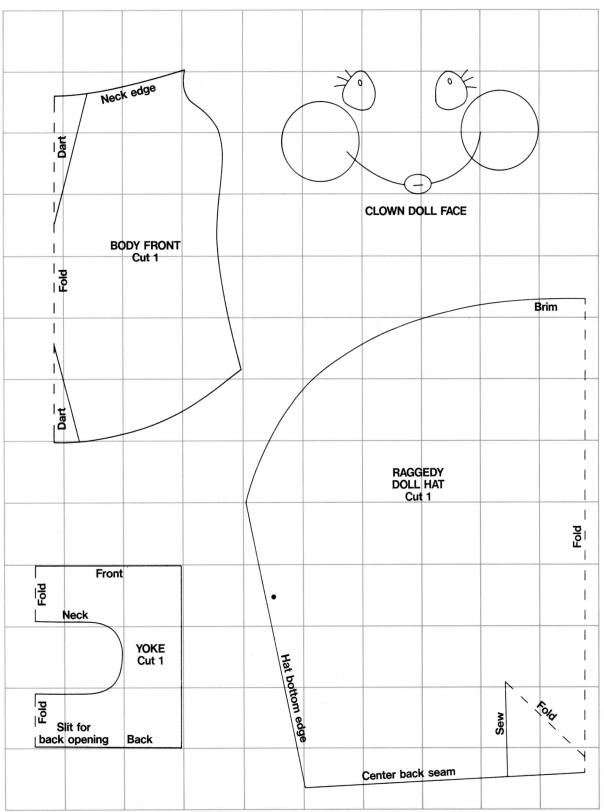

Neck edge

Dart

Fold

Dart

BODY FRONT
Cut 1

CLOWN DOLL FACE

Brim

RAGGEDY
DOLL HAT
Cut 1

Fold

Front

Fold

Neck

YOKE
Cut 1

Fold

Slit for
back opening

Back

Hat bottom edge

Sew

Fold

Center back seam

1 Square = 1 Inch

Stockings Full of Memories

With a tiny front pocket, each of these nursery-rhyme stockings has a special place for an extra holiday treat.

MATERIALS
½ yard of red calico for *each* stocking

Calico scraps in various colors for appliqués

½ yard of interfacing

Scraps of fusible webbing for appliqués

Scraps of ribbon and eyelet for goose design

INSTRUCTIONS
First, enlarge the stocking and cuff patterns, *opposite,* onto paper. Transfer stocking pattern onto red calico. Cut two stocking pieces (front and back) from *both* the red calico and interfacing.

Baste interfacing to wrong side of stocking pieces. Cut the cuff and hanging loop from contrasting fabrics, referring to photograph for ideas.

Cutting out the appliqués
TEDDY BEAR STOCKING: Cut the bear and two bear pockets from brown small-scale print; balloon from white Christmas print; and heart from red pindot fabric.

GOOSE STOCKING: Cut the body and two wing pockets from solid white fabric; bill and feet from yellow calico; and the space between the feet from the same calico used for the stocking.

COTTAGE STOCKING: Cut the cottage roof and door from green-and-white stripe; gable from green calico; cottage front from red-on-white pindot; cottage side from white Christmas print; pocket from yellow calico; and tree from another green calico.

Stitching the appliqués
Cut webbing for each appliqué. Following manufacturer's instructions, affix appliqués to background fabric as directed *below.* Using thread colors to match the appliqués (unless otherwise noted), machine-satin-stitch over the raw edges of appliqués as follows.

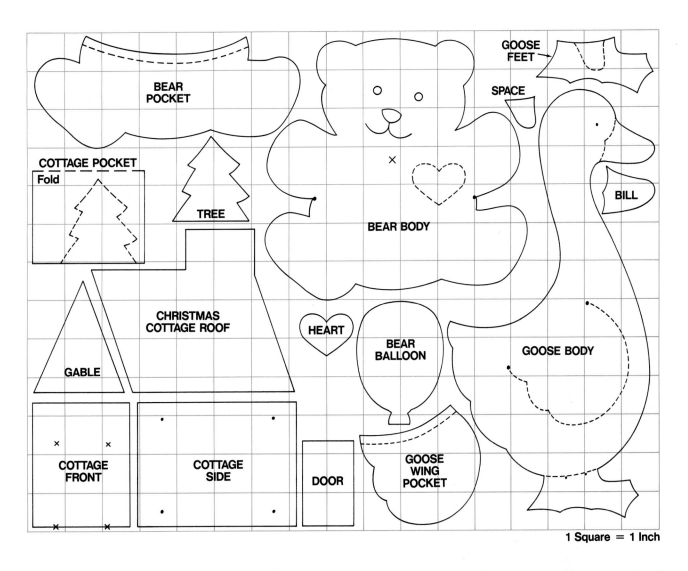

1 Square = 1 Inch

TEDDY BEAR STOCKING: Appliqué heart to bear. Place the pocket pieces right sides together; stitch along the top edge only. Turn to the right side and press.

Place the pocket atop the bear body; trim raw edges so shapes are identical, then baste in place. Machine-embroider the facial details with white satin stitches. Using white thread, appliqué the bear and balloon to the stocking front; machine-stitch the balloon string. Tack small bow to neck.

GOOSE STOCKING: Pin and baste a small length of eyelet to the right side of one wing (pocket) piece along the top edge. Place both wing pieces together, right sides facing. Stitch along the top edge only, then turn and press.

Stuff wing lightly with polyester fiberfill; machine-satin-stitch along top and sides to goose body.

Using green thread, embroider a French knot eye. Appliqué goose body to stocking front. Affix red space between feet, then affix feet and bill to goose. Add red-and-green-striped ribbon bow at neck.

COTTAGE STOCKING: Use green thread to appliqué all the pieces. Appliqué tree to one half of window (pocket). Fold in half; stitch to cottage side. Appliqué door to front. Appliqué roof, gable, and house front and side.

Assembling the stockings

Note: Stitch the stockings using ½-inch seams throughout.

With right sides together, stitch wide edge of one cuff to top of stocking front; turn and press. Repeat for stocking back.

With right sides facing, stitch the stocking front to back. Clip curves; turn and press. Turn back

cuff; blindstitch inner edge of cuff to inside of stocking. For the hanging loop, fold long edges of loop piece to center; sew. Fold in half; tack to stocking top.

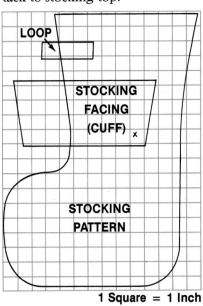

1 Square = 1 Inch

Santa Claus and the Mouse

One Christmas, when Santa Claus
    Came to a certain house,
To fill the children's stocking there,
    He found a little mouse.

"A Merry Christmas, little friend,"
    Said Santa good and kind.
"The same to you, sir," said the mouse,
    "I thought you wouldn't mind,

If I should stay awake tonight
    And watch you for a while."
"You're very welcome, little mouse,"
    Said Santa, with a smile.

And then he filled the stockings up
    Before the mouse could wink—
From toe to top, from top to toe,
    There wasn't left a chink.

"Now they won't hold another thing,"
    Said Santa Claus with pride.
A twinkle came in mouse's eyes,
    But humbly he replied:

"It's not polite to contradict—
    Your pardon I implore—
But in the fullest stocking there
    I could put one thing more."

"Oh, ho!" laughed Santa. "Silly mouse,
    Don't I know how to pack?
By filling stockings all these years
    I should have learned the knack."

And then he took the stocking down
    From where it hung so high,
And said, "Now put in one thing more,
    I give you leave to try."

The mousie chuckled to himself,
    And then he softly stole
Right to the stocking's crowded toe
    And gnawed a little hole!

"Now, if you please, good Santa Claus,
    I've put in one thing more,
For you will own that little hole
    Was not in there before."

How Santa Claus did laugh and laugh!
    And then he gaily spoke,
"Well, you shall have a Christmas cheese
    For that nice little joke!"

If you don't think this story is true,
    Why, I can show to you
The very stocking with the hole
    The little mouse gnawed through!

—Emilie Poulsson

Soft and Furry Christmas Friends

Bedecked in stylish scarves and hats, this polar-bear trio
and snowy bear will make dreams of a white Christmas
come true. For children of all ages, they'll become
favorite friends all year long.

Polar-Bear Toys And Snow Bear

Polar bears are 18, 24, and 26 inches tall. Snow bear is 24 inches tall.

MATERIALS *(for one bear)*
Bear
½ yard of white fake fur
Two ½-inch-diameter shank buttons (eyes)
No. 5 black pearl cotton
Scraps of tan leather (footpads)
1 pound of polyester fiberfill
White carpet thread; curved needle
Navy beans; toothbrush
Clothing
⅔ yard of sweatshirt fabric
1¼ yards of cord (drawstring)
Two belt eyelets; eyelet tool
Snow Bear
⅔ yard of fleece
½ yard of knit fabric (hat)
7x54-inch piece of knit fabric (scarf)
Tassel
Two ½-inch-diameter shank buttons
Black pearl cotton thread
White carpet thread
3 pounds of polyester fiberfill
Curved needle
Beans; hot-glue gun or glue
Glitter spray; white glitter

INSTRUCTIONS
Note: Use ½-inch seam allowances throughout.

For Bear
Enlarge the patterns, *pages 26–27,* onto paper. Cut out the body sections from fur.

HEAD: With right sides facing, sew fronts together at center front; clip curves. Sew front and back together at side seams. Turn; stuff firmly.

With long, doubled carpet thread, sew eyes in place. Sew two ear pieces together, right sides facing. Turn, stuff, and sew closed. Sew ears in place.

Clip the fur to measure ½ inch on ear fronts and muzzle. Using a double strand of pearl cotton, stitch the nose and mouth with outline stitches.

BODY: With right sides facing, sew fronts together at center seams; sew front to back, leaving marked openings and neck unstitched. Match dots; pin and sew the footpads in place. Turn bear right side out.

Fill feet with beans; stuff legs to dotted lines (see pattern). Hand-sew across tops of legs to create joints. Stuff arms; hand-stitch as for leg joints. Stuff firmly.

Turn under the raw edges of neck and sew to body, using carpet thread and a curved needle. Stitch twice to reinforce.

Clothing
Enlarge the patterns, *pages 28–29,* onto paper; cut out. From sweatshirt fabric, cut out the jacket pattern pieces.

Turn under top, short side, and curved edge of pocket; edge-stitch. Match front and bottom edges to jacket front and stitch in place, leaving curved edge open. Repeat for the remaining pocket.

With right sides facing, sew shoulder seams. Turn under raw edges of armholes and stitch. Join side seams. Finish front and bottom edges as for armholes.

Lay hood/lining flat and refold along line A with right sides facing. Sew both center back seams.

Turn; push lining half to inside of hood, matching center back seams. Sew hood to neck edge, leaving lining free. Insert eyelets at Xs on hood only.

Fold lining raw edge under; blindstitch. For casing, sew ½ inch from fold on front edge of hood. Insert cord and knot ends.

For Snow Bear
BOTTOM SECTION: Fold a 15x30-inch piece of fleece in half to form a square. Using ½-inch seam allowances throughout, sew the edges together opposite the fold. Turn, forming a tube.

continued

Using carpet thread, run a gathering stitch around one end. Gather tightly; secure with thread. Stuff firmly, weighting the center of the bottom section with a bag of beans. Gather top and tie off.

CENTER SECTION: Fold a 13x26-inch piece of fleece in half; finish as for the bottom section (see instructions on *page 24*).

HEAD: Use pattern for Mama Bear's head (see bear instructions, *page 24*) for snow bear's head, cutting pattern pieces from fleece instead of fur fabric.

Sew head in place over gathered portion of center. Position center on bottom section; glue. Stitch sections together.

Spray snow bear with glitter spray and sprinkle with glitter.

For Snow Bear Clothing

Cut out two hat sections. Sew together along side A, right sides facing. Fold lengthwise and sew B seam, leaving an opening for turning. Turn; sew closed. Push lining inside hat. Attach tassel to top.

With right sides facing, fold scarf fabric in half lengthwise. Stitch diagonally across each end and along the length of scarf, leaving an opening for turning. Turn; sew closed.

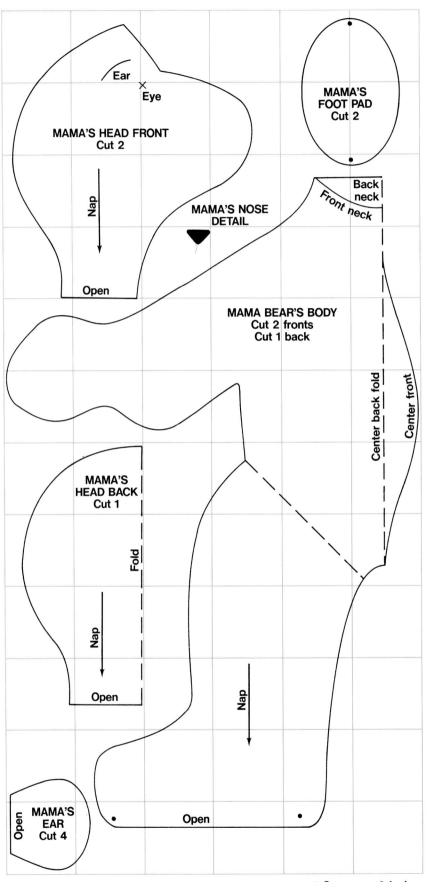

1 Square = 2 Inches

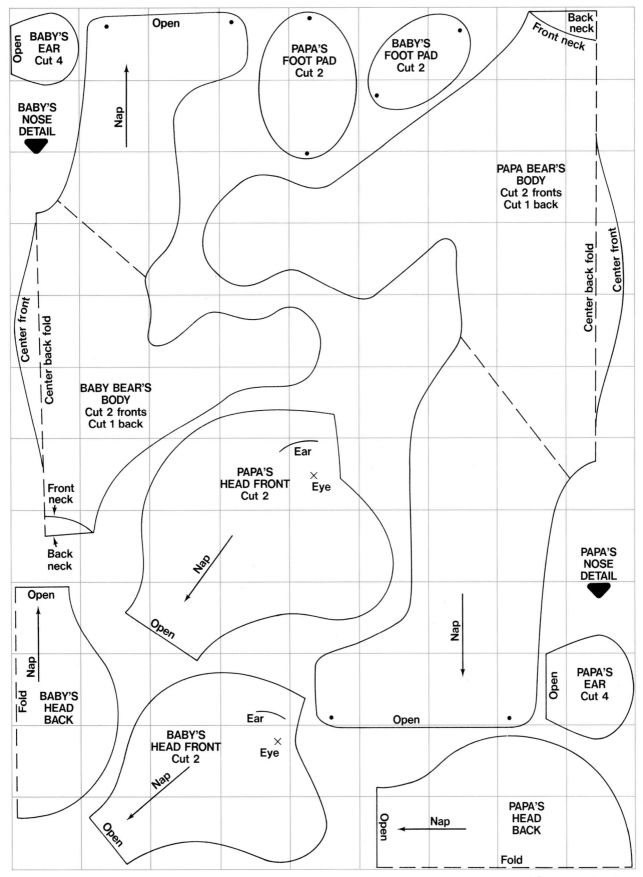

BABY'S EAR Cut 4

Open

Open

BABY'S NOSE DETAIL

Nap

PAPA'S FOOT PAD Cut 2

BABY'S FOOT PAD Cut 2

Back neck

Front neck

PAPA BEAR'S BODY
Cut 2 fronts
Cut 1 back

Center back fold

Center front

Center front

Center back fold

BABY BEAR'S BODY
Cut 2 fronts
Cut 1 back

Ear

PAPA'S HEAD FRONT Cut 2

× Eye

PAPA'S NOSE DETAIL

Front neck

Back neck

Nap

Nap

Open

Open

Nap

Fold

BABY'S HEAD BACK

Open

Ear

BABY'S HEAD FRONT Cut 2

× Eye

Nap

Open

Open

Nap

PAPA'S EAR Cut 4

Open

Open

Nap

PAPA'S HEAD BACK

Fold

1 Square = 2 Inches

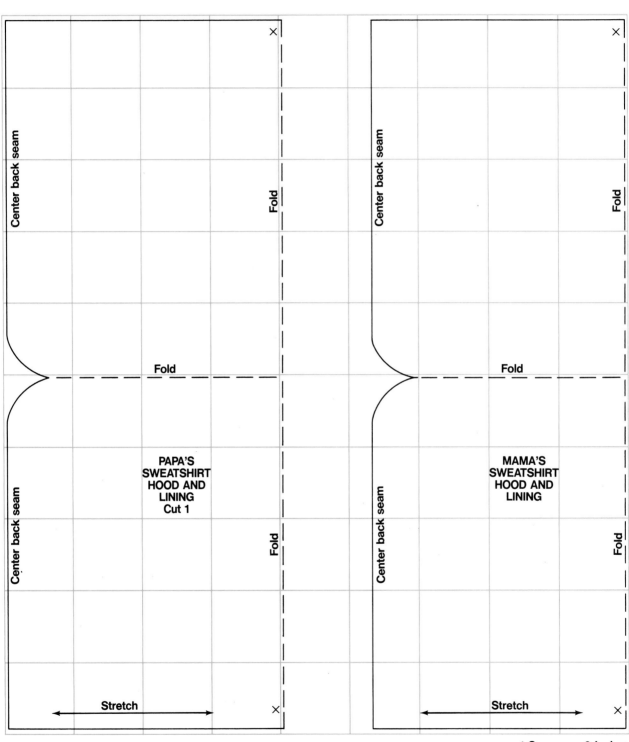

Center back seam

Fold

Fold

**PAPA'S
SWEATSHIRT
HOOD AND
LINING
Cut 1**

Center back seam

Fold

Center back seam

Fold

Fold

**MAMA'S
SWEATSHIRT
HOOD AND
LINING**

Center back seam

Fold

Stretch

Stretch

1 Square = 2 Inches

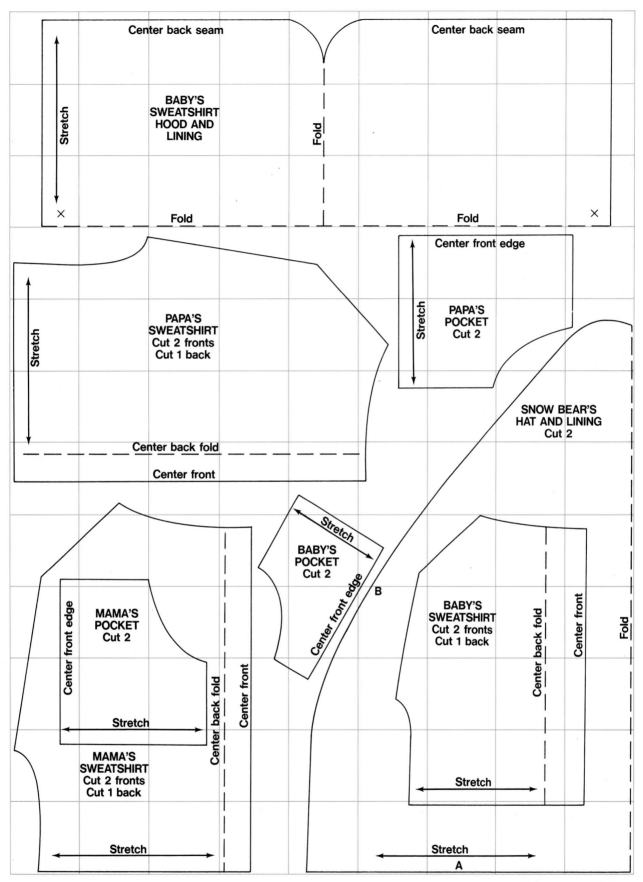

Center back seam

Center back seam

BABY'S
SWEATSHIRT
HOOD AND
LINING

Stretch

Fold

Fold

×

Fold

×

PAPA'S
SWEATSHIRT
Cut 2 fronts
Cut 1 back

Stretch

Center back fold

Center front

Center front edge

PAPA'S
POCKET
Cut 2

Stretch

SNOW BEAR'S
HAT AND LINING
Cut 2

MAMA'S
POCKET
Cut 2

Center front edge

Stretch

MAMA'S
SWEATSHIRT
Cut 2 fronts
Cut 1 back

Center back fold

Center front

Stretch

BABY'S
POCKET
Cut 2

Stretch

Center front edge

B

BABY'S
SWEATSHIRT
Cut 2 fronts
Cut 1 back

Center back fold

Center front

Fold

Stretch

Stretch

Stretch

A

1 Square = 2 Inches

31

A Toddler's Teddy Bear Book

Introduce a toddler to
the pleasures of reading
with this fully washable
teddy bear book.

3 Three keys

4 Four balloons

Teddy Bear Counting Book

The dimensions of the finished book are 11¼x13½ inches.

MATERIALS
For the pages
14x24-inch pieces of 14-count Aida cloth in the following amounts: Three pieces of pink; one piece *each* of light blue, yellow, and green

DMC Size 3 pearl cotton in No. 666 red, No. 976 light brown, No. 703 green, No. 899 rose, No. 972 yellow, No. 798 blue, No. 801 dark brown, No. 738 beige, and No. 310 black

Graph paper

Rickrack in pastel colors (1¼ yards for each page)

Tapestry needle

For the cover
⅞ yard of striped, plaid, or print fabric for the cover and cover facing

½ yard of backing fabric

2¼ yards of purchased piping in color of your choice

½ yard of fusible interfacing

INSTRUCTIONS
To make the book pages
Locate the center of all the written lines for the book, *right,* and the center of all the bear patterns, pages 32–33. Using graph paper, center and chart the written line onto the appropriate bear pattern. Allow 20 squares between the bottom line of the number on the bear design and the top of the capital letter of the written line.

Run a basting thread through the center of each of the Aida cloth pieces, both horizontally and vertically. Then run two more basting threads vertically to divide each of the pieces into eight equal parts. You now have established

two pages with the center fold line between each of these pages for each piece of Aida cloth.

Locate the center of the bear patterns (with the written words), and begin stitching the designs in the center of *one* of the pages (two designs will be worked on one piece of Aida cloth). Work cross-stitches with one strand of pearl cotton over two squares of the Aida cloth.

For paging sequence, stitch the designs on the pages as follows, working the first number on the left side of the cloth and the second number on the right side of the cloth: Stitch the number "1" and "10" designs on the blue cloth; the "9" and "2" on the pink; the "3" and "8" on the yellow; the "7" and "4" on the pink; and the "5" and "6" on the green. One piece of pink cloth should be left unworked.

Trim all the pages to measure 13½x22½ inches, making sure *continued*

Teddy Bear Counting Book
COLOR KEY 666 ⊠ Red

1 Square = 1 Stitch

Teddy Bear Patterns

1 Square = 1 Stitch

1 Square = 1 Stitch

COLOR KEY

801 ■ Dark Brown	666 ● Red	703 ⊞ Green	738 ⊟ Beige	899 Ⅱ Rose
976 ⊠ Light Brown	798 ▲ Blue	310 ◪ Black	972 · Yellow	310 ■ Black

stitched designs are centered on each half-page, with approximately 2-inch borders all around. Sew rickrack around each design, framing each page to measure 10x11¾ inches.

Allowing ½ inch for seam margins and, with right sides facing, sew unworked pink piece to blue page, leaving an opening for turning. Stitch pink "9" and "2" page to yellow page, and stitch pink "7" and "4" page to green page.

Trim the seams; turn, press, and sew openings closed.

To make the book cover

Cut one 15½x28-inch rectangle *each* from striped or print fabric, batting, and backing fabric.

Place batting between the backing and striped fabric and baste through all thicknesses; quilt as desired. Trim the quilted piece to measure 13¾x23¼ inches. Then baste and sew the piping ¼ inch from edge of quilted top.

Cut another piece of striped fabric to fit the quilted piece and fuse it with the interfacing to the wrong side.

Allowing ¼-inch seam allowances, with right sides facing, sew quilted and fused pieces together. Leave opening for turning. Turn, press, and sew opening closed.

Open cover, center assembled pages in numerical order, and sew through all thicknesses on the center line to assemble the book. Remove all basting stitches.

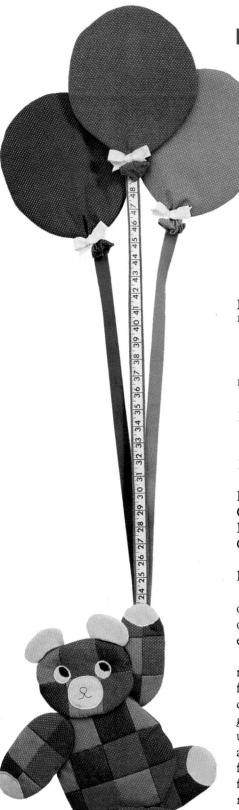

Teddy Bear Growth Chart

The perfect gift, this high-flying bear will delight any youngster on Christmas morning.

MATERIALS

½ yard *each* of red fabric (bear backing), and blue, red, and green polka-dot fabrics (balloons)

¼ yard of yellow fabric (paws, ears, eyes, muzzle)

1 yard *each* of 1-inch-wide blue, red, and green grosgrain ribbons

1 yard of ⅝-inch-wide yellow grosgrain ribbon

Blue and red embroidery floss

Quilt batting

Measuring tape

Curtain ring (hanger)

INSTRUCTIONS

Trace patterns, *right* and *opposite,* onto paper. *Note:* When cutting out pieces, add ⅜ inch all around each pattern piece for seams.

For the bear front, cut approximately thirty-six 3-inch squares from blue, red, and green polka-dot fabric. Referring to the photograph, join the squares randomly, using ⅜-inch seams. Cut the bear arms, legs, head, and body pieces from the patched fabric for the front. Cut matching pieces from red fabric for the bear back.

From yellow fabric, cut four ears and four paws. Satin-stitch the paws to the fronts of the legs and arms. Cut facial features from yellow; appliqué in place. Embroider eyes with blue floss; embroider nose and mouth with red.

PLACEMENT DIAGRAM

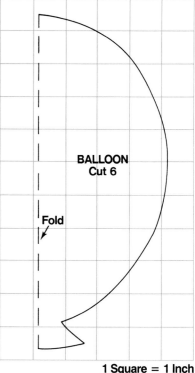

BALLOON
Cut 6

Fold

1 Square = 1 Inch

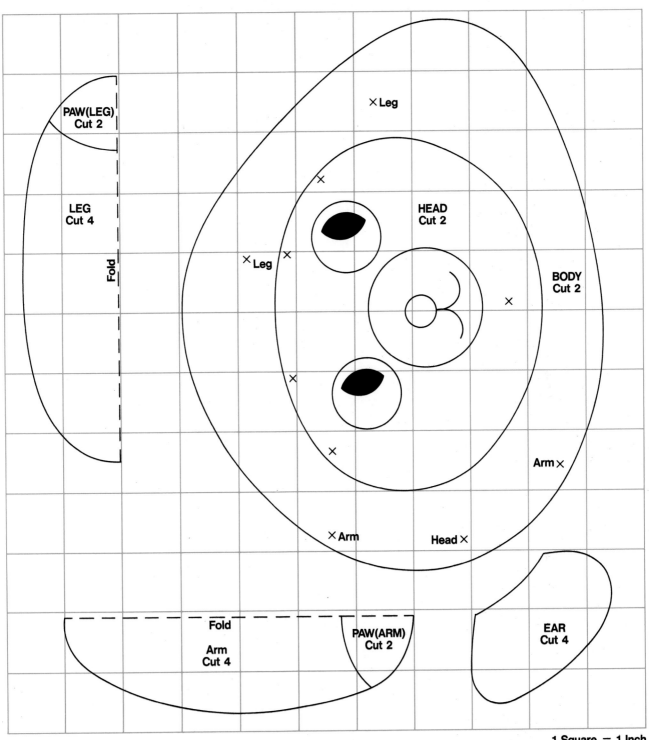

PAW(LEG)
Cut 2

LEG
Cut 4

Fold

× Leg

× Leg

× Leg

HEAD
Cut 2

BODY
Cut 2

×

Arm ×

× Arm

Head ×

Fold

Arm
Cut 4

PAW(ARM)
Cut 2

EAR
Cut 4

1 Square = 1 Inch

Back the front and back body pieces with batting. Sew the front to back, right sides facing, leaving an opening for turning. Clip, turn, and sew opening closed.

Pin ears to head front. Add batting to head front and back; sew as for body. Turn; sew opening. Sew legs and arms in same manner. Following diagram, *opposite,* tack the legs, arms, and head to body.

Cut six balloons (two of each color) from polka-dot fabric. Add 2-inch hems to balloon bottoms. Assemble balloons with batting as for bear body, leaving bottom edges open. Turn; fold hems to inside. Tie bottom of each balloon closed, using yellow ribbon.

Sew a tape measure to red ribbon. Tack ribbon to other two balloons; attach ribbons to bear's left paw. Sew a ring to the back of red balloon for hanging.

A Real Santa Claus

Santa Claus, I hang for you,
By the mantel, stockings two:
One for me and one to go
To another boy I know.

There's a chimney in the town
You have never traveled down.
Should you chance to enter there
You would find a room all bare:
Not a stocking could you spy,
Matters not how you might try;
And the shoes, you'd find are such
As no boy would care for much.
In a broken bed you'd see
Some one just about like me,
Dreaming of the pretty toys
Which you bring to other boys,
And to him a Christmas seems
Merry only in his dreams.

All he dreams then, Santa Claus,
Stuff the stocking with, because
When it's filled up to the brim
I'll be Santa Claus to him!

—Frank Dempster Sherman

Presents

I wanted a rifle for Christmas,
I wanted a bat and a ball,
I wanted some skates and a bicycle,
But I didn't want mittens at all.

I wanted a whistle
And I wanted a kite,
I wanted a pocketknife
That shut up tight.
I wanted some boots
And I wanted a kit,
But I didn't want mittens one little bit.

I told them I didn't like mittens,
I told them as plain as plain.
I told them I didn't WANT mittens,
And they've given me mittens again!

—Marchette Chute

An Alphabet Of Christmas

A is for Animals who shared the stable.
B for the Babe with their manger for cradle.
C for the Carols so blithe and gay.
D for December, the twenty-fifth day.
E for the Eve when we're all so excited.
F for the Fun when the tree's at last lighted.

G is for Goose which you all know is fat.
H is the Holly you stick in your hat.
I for the Ivy that clings to the wall.
J is for Jesus, the cause of it all.
K for the Kindness begot by this feast.
L is for Light shining way in the East.
M for the Mistletoe, all green and white.
N for the Noels we sing Christmas night.
O for the Oxen, the first to adore Him.
P for the Presents Wise Men laid before Him.

Q for the Quiet of the holy Eve
  as God's greatest blessing we all did receive.
R for the Reindeer leaping over the roofs.
S for the Stockings that Santa Claus stuffs.
T for the Toys, the Tinsel, the Tree.
U is for Us—the whole family.
V is the Visitors bringing us cheer.
W is Welcome to the happy New Year.
X Y Z bother me! So now
  to you all, wherever you be,
  a merry, merry Christmas,
  and many may you see!

Santa's Treeful of Trims

Just put on your elf thinking cap, and you can come up with cookie cutter trims that would make Santa say a cheery "Ho, ho, ho!" Ask Mom to let you borrow her cookie cutters for Christmas designs, or use our suggestions to quickly make a kitchenful of trims.

MATERIALS

Basic recipe
2 cups flour
1 cup salt
1 cup cold water

Other materials
Cookie cutters
Paraffin
Rolling pin
Small black beads
Paste food coloring
White acrylic paint
Paper clips

INSTRUCTIONS

Mix together one batch of the basic recipe, kneading the mixture until it forms a medium-stiff, smooth dough. If necessary, add more flour or water to reach the right consistency. Color some dough red and some green. Mix a second batch of the dough, adding white acrylic paint for color.

TEDDY BEARS: Use a rolling pin and a flour-covered surface to roll out the white dough to about ½ inch thickness. Using cookie cutters, cut out several bears.

Following the patterns on this page for guidance, shape little bows, leaves, and berries from red and green dough, then use them to decorate the bears. Push small black beads into the dough to form the bears' eyes.

CANDY CANES: Roll equal-size pieces of red and white dough into ropes. Referring to the photograph, *right,* twist the two ropes together. Cut the twisted strips to the desired length; bend one end to make the cane's curved top.

STOCKING: Use a rolling pin to roll out red dough and white dough to approximately ½-inch thickness. Using a cookie cutter or the pattern on this page, cut a stocking from red dough. Cut a cuff from white dough, and shape leaves and berries from green and white. Make two small candy canes as directed above.

Lay the white cuff over the top of the stocking and press in place. Using a toothpick, make dashes in the stocking along the toe and heel. Position the candy canes, leaves, and berries in place; press.

WREATHS: Cut wreaths from green dough, using a cookie cutter, drinking glass, or biscuit cutter. Decorate the wreaths with miniature bows shaped according to the bow pattern, *above.* Add miniature holly leaves and berries, if desired.

STARS: Using a cookie cutter, cut stars in a variety of colors.

Finishing the ornaments

Insert one-half of a paper clip into the top of each ornament, forming a hoop for hanging.

Lay the ornaments on foil-covered cookie sheets and bake in a 325° oven for 1 to 2 hours, or until hard. Let cool.

With help from Mom or Dad, melt the paraffin in a bowl placed in a pan of boiling water. Using a slotted spatula or spoon, dip each ornament into the melted paraffin. Transfer the ornament to a wire rack that is sitting on newspapers. Let cool.

Paper-Plate Angels

The heavenly angels pictured here are easy to make from paper plates. Make one for the treetop, and more for the windowsills or holiday table.

MATERIALS
Thin, flute-edge 9-inch
   paper plates
White crafts glue
Stapler
Kitchen spoon
Scissors
Tracing paper
Pencil
Masking tape

INSTRUCTIONS

TRACING PATTERNS: Use a soft pencil to trace the pattern, *page 46,* onto tissue paper. Then center the tissue facedown on a paper plate and tape it in place. Use the back of a spoon to rub over the pencil lines (except for the outside circle, which is shown only to help you center the design on the plate). This will transfer the pencil drawing to the plate.

Transfer the wing patterns, *page 47,* in the same way. The patterns show you where to place the edges of the wings so that the scallops of the plate become the ruffles on the wings.

Cut the line marked "cut here" from the edge of the plate up to the head. Use small scissors to cut along all solid lines. In the head area, you will see two small rectangles. Cut them out. These cutouts form the bottom shape of the hair. *Do not* cut the two dotted lines.

SHAPING THE SKIRT: Turn the plate over so that the edge curves to the inside and so all pencil marks are on the back. Hold the two skirt edges where you cut the slit and overlap them about 3 inches. Staple the edges together to hold the skirt in place. (See Drawing 1, *page 47.*)

PRAYING HANDS: Pull the angel's hands and head slightly forward. Bend arms away from *continued*

45

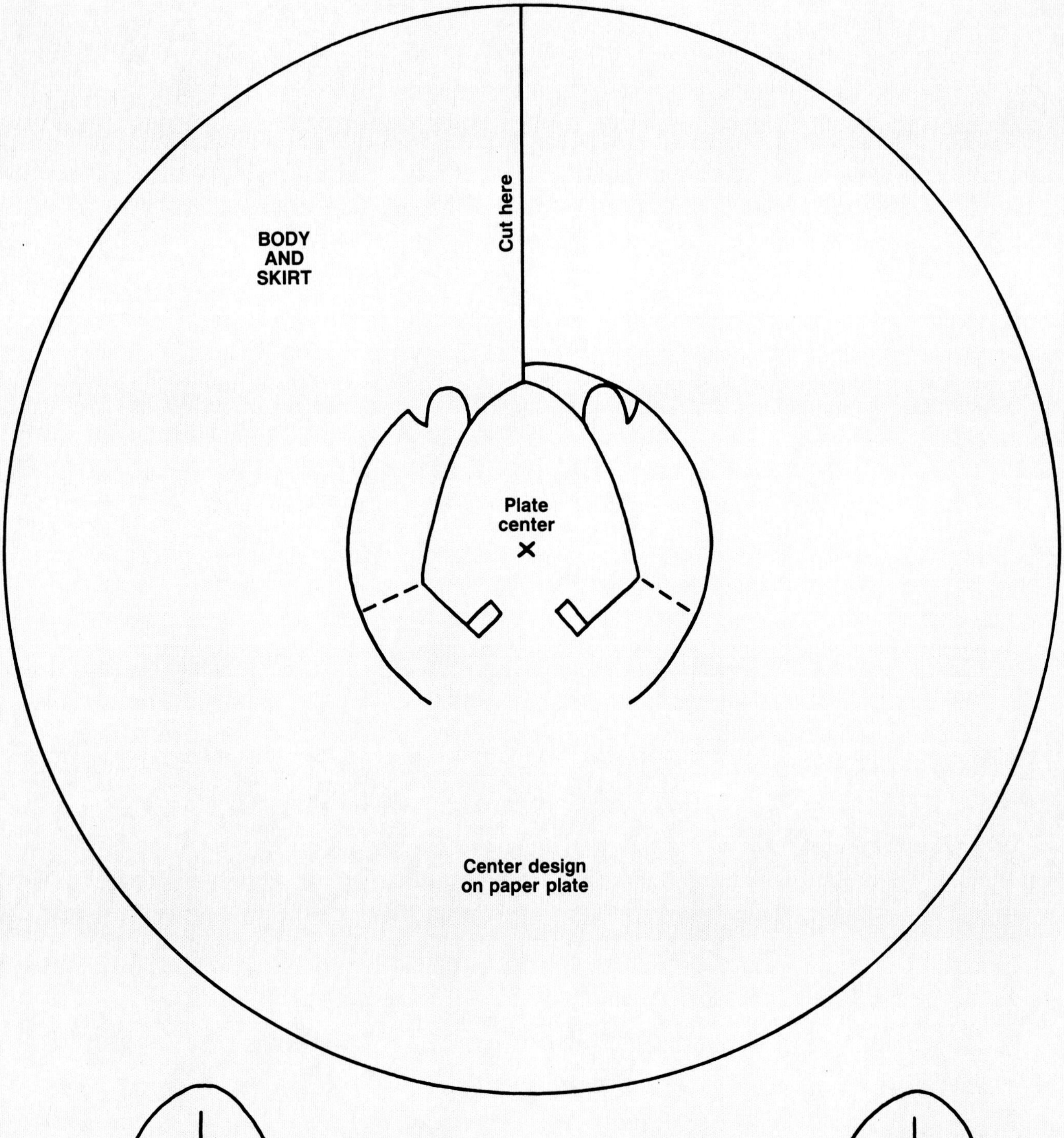

BODY
AND
SKIRT

Cut here

Plate
center
✕

Center design
on paper plate

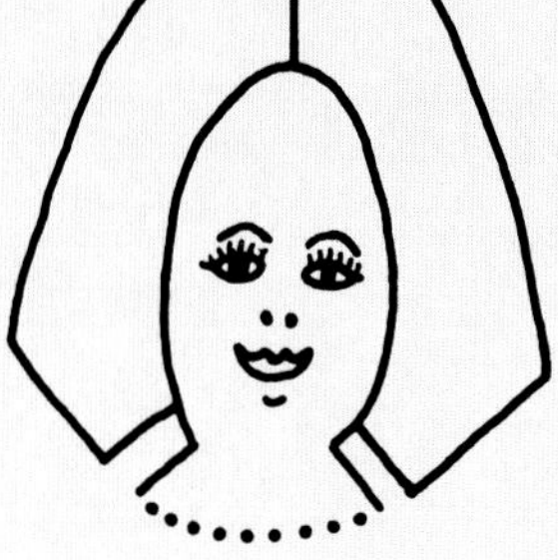

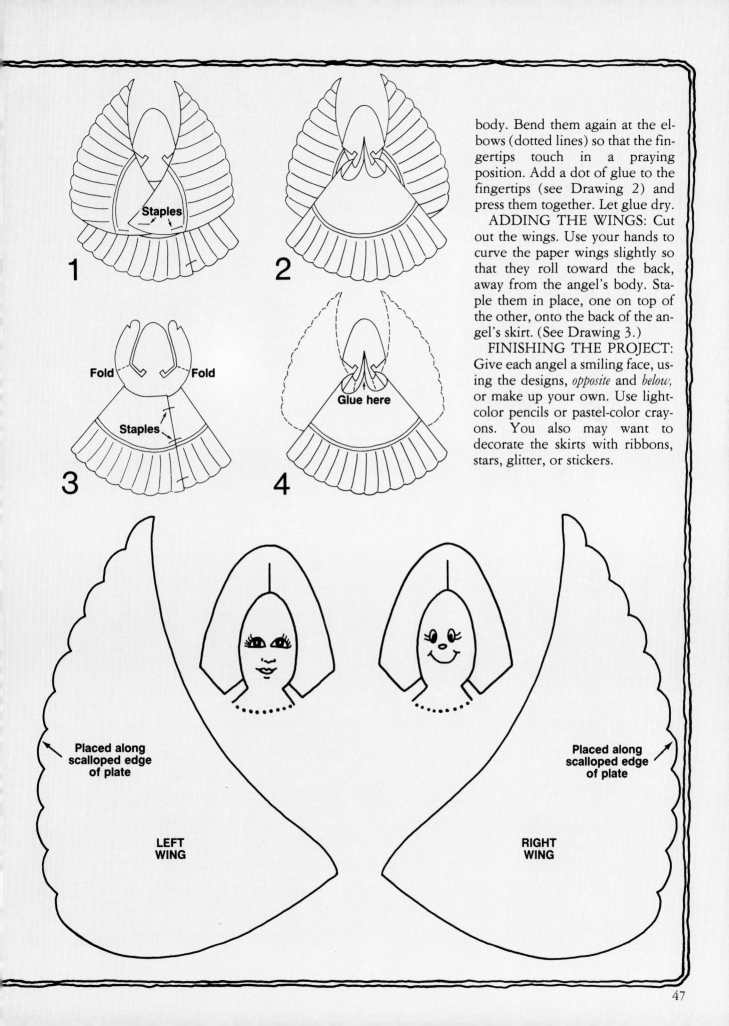

1 Staples

2

3 Fold Fold Staples

4 Glue here

body. Bend them again at the elbows (dotted lines) so that the fingertips touch in a praying position. Add a dot of glue to the fingertips (see Drawing 2) and press them together. Let glue dry.

ADDING THE WINGS: Cut out the wings. Use your hands to curve the paper wings slightly so that they roll toward the back, away from the angel's body. Staple them in place, one on top of the other, onto the back of the angel's skirt. (See Drawing 3.)

FINISHING THE PROJECT: Give each angel a smiling face, using the designs, *opposite* and *below*, or make up your own. Use light-color pencils or pastel-color crayons. You also may want to decorate the skirts with ribbons, stars, glitter, or stickers.

Placed along scalloped edge of plate

Placed along scalloped edge of plate

LEFT WING

RIGHT WING

Hang Up the Baby's Stocking

Hang up the baby's stocking;
Be sure you don't forget;
The dear little dimpled darling!
She ne'er saw Christmas yet;
But I've told her all about it,
And she opened her big blue eyes;
And I'm sure she understood it—
She looked so funny and wise.

Dear! what a tiny stocking!
It doesn't take much to hold
Such little pink toes as baby's
Away from the frost and cold;
But then for the baby's Christmas
It will never do at all!
Why, Santa wouldn't be looking
For anything half so small.

I know what will do for the baby.
I've thought of the very best plan:
I'll borrow a stocking of grandma,
The longest that ever I can;
And you'll hang it by mine, dear mother,
Right here in the corner, so,
And write a letter to Santa,
And fasten it on the toe.

Write, "This is the baby's stocking
That hangs in the corner here;
You never have seen her, Santa,
For she only came this year;
But she's just the blessedest baby!
And now before you go,
Just cram her stocking with goodies,
From the top clean down to the toe."

—*Emily Huntington Miller*

Golden Cobwebs

The Christmas tree stood by the parlor door,
　But the parlor door was locked
And the children could not get inside
　Even though they knocked.
For a Christmas tree must wait, folks say,
And not be seen till Christmas Day.
But the cat had seen the Christmas tree
　As she prowled the house by night,
And the dog had seen the Christmas tree
　By the moon's enchanting light;
And a little mouse beside her hole
Had looked at it with eyes of coal.
Even the spiders hoped to see
The secret, silent Christmas tree.
They planned, one day, to creep and crawl
Out of their cracks and up the wall
To get the highest view of all.
But just that day with mop and broom
The housemaid swept them from the room
And so the spiders could not see
The secret, silent Christmas tree.

The fairies heard the spiders weep,
　All on a winter's night,
Although their cries made softer sounds
　Than moth wings make in flight.
The fairies said: "Each living thing
That creeps, or crawls, or flaps a wing
Shall share the birthday of the King."

KUNZE

They took the spiders to the tree
    And, since they were too small
To see as far as cat or mouse,
    The fairies let them crawl
Along each twig and bending branch
    To look at every ball
And silver star and popcorn string;
And when they had seen everything
They thanked the fairies and went back
Each one to sleep inside his crack.

But, oh, the tree when they were gone
Was very sad to look upon!
Its branches were more gray than green
And little webs hung in between
That dulled the lights and all the sheen.

The fairies shook their heads and sighed,
For in their wisdom, ever wide,
They knew no housewife cared to see
Dull cobwebs on a Christmas tree.
They knew the children, too, would weep
To waken from their yuletide sleep
And glimpse a tree all bearded gray
That would not shine on Christmas Day. . . .

And so they turned the webs to gold
By waving fairy wands, I'm told;
And that is why there'll always be
Bright cobwebs on a Christmas tree.
                              —*Rowena Bennett*

St. Nick's Gingerbread Village

The Grimm brothers made the gingerbread house
famous in their fairy tale "Hansel and Gretel." Now
create your own never-never land with this gingerbread
village and delightful gingerbread teddy bears.

Tiny Gingerbread Town

5 cups all-purpose flour
2 teaspoons ground ginger
1 teaspoon baking soda
1 teaspoon ground cinnamon
½ teaspoon salt
1 cup margarine *or* butter
1 cup sugar
1 cup molasses
   Snow Frosting
   Green food coloring
   Assorted candies
   Mixed whole nuts
   Powdered sugar

Make patterns by tracing the figures on page 55 onto cardboard and cutting them out. Set aside.

Mix flour, ginger, baking soda, cinnamon, and salt. In a large mixer bowl beat margarine till softened. Add sugar and beat till fluffy. Add molasses and beat well. Gradually beat in flour mixture, working in last part by hand.

Divide dough into thirds. Roll each third ¼ inch thick directly onto an ungreased cookie sheet,*

placing waxed paper over dough to prevent sticking to the rolling pin. Cut around patterns as shown on page 54. Lift off scraps and reserve. Cut *half* of the tree pieces and *one* of the steeple pieces in half from top to bottom. Give roofs and walls designs by scoring with a knive or pressing with the tip of a spoon or one side of a tiny hors d'oeuvres cutter. Reroll scraps to cut number of pieces shown on page 55.

Bake in a 375° oven for 9 to 11 minutes or till done. While cookies are still hot on cookie sheet, trim straight edges of trees, steeple, and building pieces to straighten. Remove and cool.

Assemble trees as shown on page 54. Decorate with some of the Snow Frosting tinted with green food coloring and attach candies. Assemble buildings with Snow Frosting as shown on page 54. Let dry and decorate with frosting and candies. For church, attach two steeple halves to whole steeple piece at right angles with frosting. Attach a small candy to steeple top. Secure steeple to roof with frosting.

Arrange buildings and trees on a large foil-covered piece of cardboard. For pond, cut a piece of

nonabsorbent colored paper into desired shape and attach to foil. With a star tip, pipe frosting around edge. (Or, pipe frosting directly onto foil for pond outline.) For fence, use a writing tip to pipe a ¾-inch-wide strip of frosting on foil, then press in nuts. Repeat layers till fence is desired height, ending with frosting. Sift powdered sugar over town for snow. Arrange candies in front of buildings for walks. Makes 3 buildings and 8 trees.

Snow Frosting: In a large mixer bowl beat 1½ cups *shortening* and 1½ teaspoons *vanilla* for 30 seconds. Gradually beat in 3½ cups sifted *powdered sugar.* Add 3 tablespoons *milk.* Gradually beat in 3½ cups more sifted *powdered sugar* and enough *milk* (3 to 4 tablespoons) to make frosting of piping consistency.

*If making a stained-glass window in church front, cover the cookie sheet with foil before rolling out dough. Cut a hole in the dough with a tiny hors d'oeuvres cutter or knife and fill hole with crushed *clear hard candies.* Bake as directed above.

Cutting out the dough

Roll dough directly onto a cookie sheet. (Do not flour the cookie sheet.) Place a damp towel under the cookie sheet to prevent sliding as you roll.

Place the patterns ½ inch apart on dough to allow for spreading during baking. Cut around patterns with a sharp knife, fitting as many pieces on a cookie sheet as you can.

1

2

Assembling the trees

For each tree, pipe or spread frosting onto the straight edge of two tree halves. Attach to a whole tree piece so the halves are at right angles to the whole. Let dry before decorating.

Tint some frosting with green food coloring and pipe onto trees with a star tip. Attach candies with more frosting.

3

Assembling the buildings

Pipe frosting along the bottom edge of the side- and endpieces of each building. Place the pieces, frosting side down, on the round base. With a writing tip, join the four walls by piping frosting along the corner edges where the walls meet. Let dry before adding the roof.

When you're ready to roof, pipe frosting along the top edges of all the standing walls. Attach one roof piece, then the other.

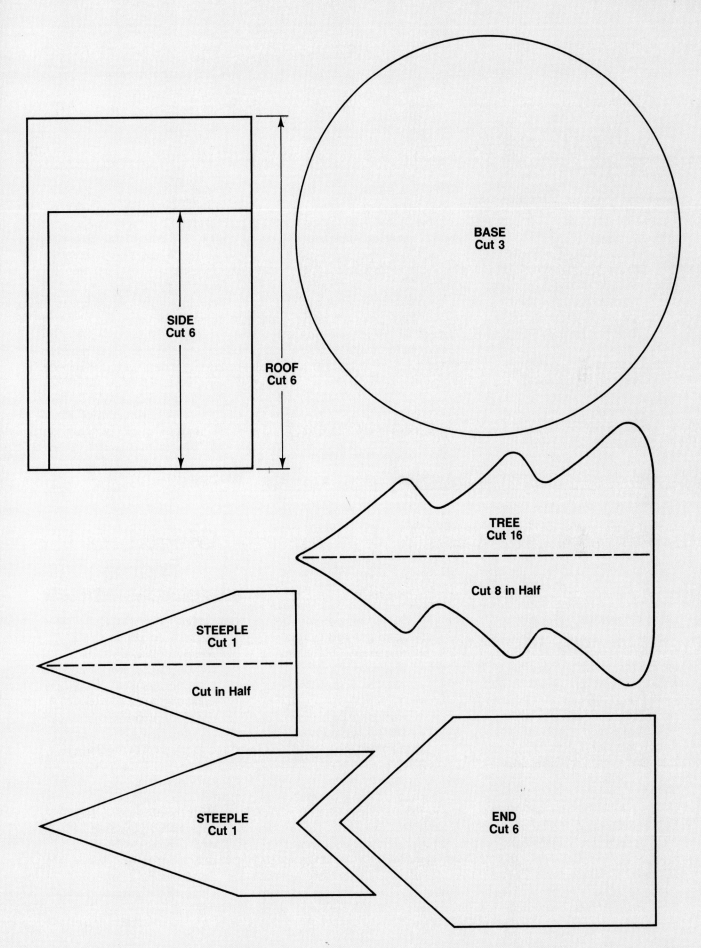

SIDE
Cut 6

ROOF
Cut 6

BASE
Cut 3

TREE
Cut 16

Cut 8 in Half

STEEPLE
Cut 1

Cut in Half

STEEPLE
Cut 1

END
Cut 6

Gingerbread Teddy Bears

Pictured opposite.

    1 cup margarine *or* butter
    ⅔ cup packed brown sugar
    ⅔ cup dark corn syrup, light
        corn syrup, *or* molasses
    4 cups all-purpose flour
    1½ teaspoons ground
        cinnamon
    1 teaspoon ground ginger
    ¾ teaspoon baking soda
    ½ teaspoon ground cloves
    1 beaten egg
    1½ teaspoons vanilla
        Miniature semisweet
        chocolate pieces
        Decorating Icing (optional)

In a saucepan combine margarine, brown sugar, and corn syrup. Cook and stir over medium heat till margarine is melted and sugar is dissolved. Pour into a large mixing bowl and cool 5 minutes. Meanwhile, combine flour, cinnamon, ginger, soda, and cloves.

Add egg and vanilla to margarine mixture and mix well. Add the flour mixture and beat till well mixed. Divide the dough in half. Cover and chill at least 2 hours or overnight.

To make each teddy bear, shape dough into one 1-inch ball, one ¾-inch ball, six ½-inch balls, and five ¼-inch balls. On an ungreased cookie sheet flatten the 1-inch ball to ½ inch for body. Attach the ¾-inch ball for head and flatten to ½ inch. Attach the ½-inch balls for arms, legs, and ears. Place one of the ¼-inch balls on head for nose. Arrange remaining ¼-inch balls atop ends of arms and legs for

paws. Use miniature chocolate pieces for eyes and navel.

Bake in a 350° oven for 8 to 10 minutes or till done. Carefully remove and cool. If desired, pipe on bow ties with Decorating Icing. Makes 16.

Decorating Icing: Combine ½ cup sifted *powdered sugar* and enough *milk or light cream* (about 2 teaspoons) to make of piping consistency. Tint with one or two drops *food coloring.*

Gingerbread Spritz

These molasses and spice cookies have a cakier texture than traditional Spritz.

    2¾ cups all-purpose flour
    ¾ teaspoon baking powder
    ½ teaspoon ground nutmeg
    ½ teaspoon ground cinnamon
    ¼ teaspoon ground cloves
    ¼ teaspoon ground ginger
    1 cup margarine *or* butter
    ¼ cup molasses
    ¼ cup packed brown sugar
    1 egg
    1 teaspoon vanilla
        Powdered Sugar Glaze
        (optional)

In a large mixing bowl stir together the flour, baking powder, nutmeg, cinnamon, cloves, and ginger. Set aside.

In a large mixer bowl beat margarine or butter on medium speed of an electric mixer for 30 seconds. Add molasses and brown sugar and beat till combined. Add

egg and vanilla and beat well. Gradually stir in flour mixture till combined. *Do not chill dough.*

Pack the dough into a cookie press. Force the dough through the cookie press onto an ungreased cookie sheet.

Bake in a 400° oven for 6 to 8 minutes or till edges are firm but not brown. Remove; cool completely on wire racks. If desired, drizzle cookies with Powdered Sugar Glaze. Makes about 48.

Powdered Sugar Glaze: In a small mixing bowl combine 1 cup sifted *powdered sugar,* ¼ teaspoon *vanilla,* and enough *milk* to make of drizzling consistency (about 1½ tablespoons).

Gingerbread People

    1¾ cups all-purpose flour
    ¾ cup whole wheat flour
    ¾ teaspoon baking soda
    ½ teaspoon ground ginger
    ½ teaspoon ground cinnamon
    ¼ teaspoon ground allspice
    ¼ teaspoon ground nutmeg
    ½ cup shortening
    ½ cup packed brown sugar
    1 egg
    ⅓ cup molasses
    3 tablespoons honey
    1 tablespoon lemon juice
    2 cups sifted powdered sugar
    1 egg white
    2 teaspoons lemon juice
        Food coloring (optional)
        Decorative candies
        (optional)

In a medium mixing bowl stir together all-purpose flour, whole wheat flour, baking soda, ginger, cinnamon, allspice, and nutmeg. Set aside.

Beat shortening for 30 seconds. Add brown sugar and beat till fluffy. Add egg, molasses, honey, and the 1 tablespoon lemon juice; beat well. Gradually add flour mixture, beating till combined. (You may have to stir in the last part of the flour mixture with a wooden spoon.) Divide dough in half. Cover and chill about 3 hours or till easy to handle.

Grease a cookie sheet. Set aside. On a floured surface roll dough ⅛ inch thick. Cut with 3- to 4-inch people cookie cutters. Place 1 inch apart on prepared cookie sheet. Bake in a 375° oven for 4 to 5 minutes or till edges are firm and bottoms lightly browned.

Cool for 1 minute. Remove; cool completely on wire racks.

For frosting, beat together powdered sugar, egg white, and the 2 teaspoons lemon juice. If desired, stir several drops of food coloring into frosting. Spread frosting over cookies. If desired, decorate with candies. Makes about 54.

A Gift for Mr. Guerney

—by Deborah Apy

There was once a young girl named Charlotte who especially liked an old man named Mr. Guerney who lived about a mile away from her. So Charlotte made four gingerbread men to take to him for Christmas.

Charlotte carefully wrapped the gingerbread men in red and green tissue, put on her warm coat and scarf and mittens, and left on a blustery day for Mr. Guerney's house. She walked a little ways until she saw a dog sitting in the snow. "Owwoooo," howled the dog, and he looked so cold that Charlotte felt sorry for him, so she gave him a gingerbread man to eat.

Now Charlotte had three gingerbread men for Mr. Guerney. But soon she heard a loud chattering and twirping. Walking up to a snow-filled bush she say Mrs. Bloom's big old Tomcat circling around on the ground, eyeing a chickadee in the branches. "Oh, go on!" Charlotte chased the Tom away. She wondered why the chickadee wouldn't fly and thought maybe he needed some food. So Charlotte crumbled up a gingerbread man and left it beneath the bush for the bird.

Now Charlotte had two gingerbread men for Mr. Guerney. She had almost reached his house when she heard some sniffles and whimpers. Then she saw little, four-year-old Lorry Simpson crying in her front yard. Lorry's big brother, David, had gone sledding and told her she was too little to go. "Oh, dear," said Charlotte, and she gave Lorry a gingerbred man, the cutest one with the red eyes and the raisin nose.

Now Charlotte had only one gingerbread man left, and she had meant to bring four! Oh no, she thought, one gingerbread man wasn't much of a gift for such a good friend as Mr. Guerney.

Mr. Guerney smiled broadly when he saw Charlotte. "Come in, come in," he said. His eyes twinkled as she told him she only had one gingerbread man for him, but she had started out with four. He fixed them some hot chocolate to enjoy as they shared the last gingerbread man, and Charlotte told Mr. Guerney about the dog and the chickadee and little Lorry Simpson. They had a very nice visit, and when Charlotte left Mr. Guerney said, "Charlotte, you gave me one gingerbread man and three stories. That's better than four gingerbread men. In fact, that's the best present I've had all year."

Charlotte smiled happily. Maybe, she thought, next year I'll make five gingerbread men.

Sweets for Santa

It's always such a debate—what to leave for Santa on Christmas Eve. But when you leave him cookies and candies like Spritz and Walnut Caramels, we guarantee old St. Nick will lick up every crumb. (And don't forget a carrot for Rudolf!)

Pizzelles

Bake these Italian wafer cookies in a pizzelle (piz-ZEL-ee) iron. Pictured opposite.

  2 cups all-purpose flour
  1 tablespoon baking powder
1½ teaspoons ground nutmeg
  ½ teaspoon ground
      cardamom
  3 eggs
  ¾ cup sugar
  ⅓ cup margarine *or* butter,
      melted and cooled
  2 teaspoons vanilla

Stir together flour, baking powder, nutmeg, and cardamom. In a small mixer bowl beat eggs with an electric mixer on high speed about 4 minutes or till thick and lemon colored. With mixer on medium speed, gradually beat in sugar. Beat in cooled, melted margarine or butter and vanilla. Add flour mixture and beat on low speed till combined.

Heat pizzelle iron on range-top over medium heat (or heat an electric pizzelle iron according to manufacturer's directions) till a drop of water sizzles on the grid.

Reduce heat to medium-low. Place a slightly rounded tablespoon of batter in the center of the round grid. Squeeze lid to close. Bake for 30 to 60 seconds or till golden, turning iron once. (Or, use an electric pizzelle iron according to manufacturer's directions.) Turn wafer out onto a paper towel to cool. Repeat with remaining batter. Makes 18.

Snowmen

Pictured opposite.

  1 cup margarine *or* butter
  ½ cup sugar
  1 teaspoon vanilla
2¼ cups all-purpose flour
      Miniature semisweet
        chocolate pieces
      Powdered Sugar Icing
      Thin ribbon *or* shoestring
        licorice
      Large gumdrops
      Powdered sugar
      Food coloring (optional)

In a large mixer bowl beat margarine or butter till softened. Add sugar and beat till fluffy. Beat in vanilla. Add flour and beat till well mixed. For each snowman, shape dough into three balls: one 1-inch ball, one ¾-inch ball, and one ½-inch ball.

Place balls on an ungreased cookie sheet in decreasing sizes with sides touching. Press together slightly. Insert two chocolate pieces in smallest ball for eyes; one in middle-size ball and two in largest ball for buttons. Bake in a 325° oven for 18 to 20 minutes or till done. Remove and cool.

Prepared Powdered Sugar Icing. Tie a 6-inch piece of ribbon or licorice around the neck of each snowman. For each hat, sprinkle additional sugar on a cutting board. Place one gumdrop on sugared board and sprinkle with more sugar. With a rolling pin, roll gumdrop into an oval about ⅛ inch thick. Curve to form a cone and press together to seal. If desired, bend up edge for a brim. Attach to head with the icing. Lightly sprinkle snowmen with powdered sugar. If broom is desired, tint remaining icing with food coloring and pipe onto cookies. Makes about 24.

Powdered Sugar Icing: Combine ¾ cup sifted *powdered sugar* and enough *milk* (about 1 tablespoon) to make it spreadable.

Candy Canes

Pictured on page 57.

1 cup margarine *or* butter
1 cup sifted powdered sugar
1 egg
½ teaspoon vanilla
½ teaspoon peppermint
    extract
2½ cups all-purpose flour
½ teaspoon red food coloring
    Peppermint Glaze
    (optional)

In a large mixer bowl beat margarine or butter till softened. Add powdered sugar and beat till fluffy. Add egg, vanilla, peppermint extract, and dash salt. Beat well. Add flour and beat till well combined. Divide dough in half. Stir food coloring into one half. Cover each half and chill about 30 minutes or till easy to handle.

For each cookie, on a lightly floured surface shape a teaspoonful of uncolored dough into a 4-inch rope. Repeat with a teaspoonful of red dough. Place ropes side by side and twist together. Pinch ends to seal. Form twisted ropes into a cane. Place canes 2 inches apart on an ungreased cookie sheet.

Bake in a 375° oven for 8 to 10 minutes or till done. Remove and cool. If desired, brush with Peppermint Glaze. Makes 48.

Peppermint Glaze: Stir together 1 cup sifted *powdered sugar,* ¼ teaspoon *peppermint extract,* and enough *water* (4 to 5 teaspoons) to make of brushing consistency.

Peppernuts

These spicy nuggets are about as big as the tip of your little finger. Once you start munching, it's hard to stop. Pictured on page 57.

¾ cup sugar
⅔ cup dark corn syrup
¼ cup milk
¼ cup shortening
1 teaspoon anise extract
½ teaspoon baking powder
½ teaspoon vanilla
¼ teaspoon salt
¼ teaspoon ground cinnamon
¼ teaspoon ground
    cardamom
¼ teaspoon ground cloves
3⅓ cups all-purpose flour
    Sifted powdered sugar

In a large saucepan combine sugar, corn syrup, milk, and shortening. Bring to boiling. Remove from heat and cool about 15 minutes. Stir in anise extract, baking powder, vanilla, salt, cinnamon, cardamom, and cloves. Stir in flour till well combined. Cover and chill about 2 hours or till dough is easy to handle.

Divide dough into 24 equal parts. On a surface dusted lightly with sifted powdered sugar, roll each part of dough into a ¼-inch-thick rope. Cut into pieces about ⅜ inch long. Place 1 inch apart on a greased cookie sheet.

Bake in a 375° oven for 10 to 12 minutes or till done. Immediately remove and cool on paper towels. Makes 8 cups of cookies.

Bready Bears

Move over Rudolf—the bready bears have arrived! Pictured opposite.

5¼ to 5½ cups all-purpose
    flour
1 package active dry yeast
1 cup milk
⅓ cup sugar
½ cup shortening
2 beaten eggs
2 tablespoons finely
    shredded orange peel
¼ cup orange juice
1 slightly beaten egg white
    Sugar Glaze
    Dried fruit *or* nuts
    (optional)

Combine *2 cups* of the flour and yeast. Heat milk, sugar, shortening, and 1 teaspoon *salt* till warm (115° to 120°); stir constantly. Add to flour mixture along with eggs, orange peel, and orange juice. Beat with an electric mixer on low speed for 30 seconds; scrape often. Beat 3 minutes at high speed. Stir in as much of the remaining flour as you can. Turn out onto a lightly floured surface. Knead in enough remaining flour to make a moderately soft dough that is smooth and elastic (3 to 5 minutes total).

Place dough in a greased bowl. Cover; let rise in a warm place till double (about 1 hour). Punch dough down. Cover and let rest 10 minutes. Divide dough in half. On a lightly floured surface roll out 1 half to ½-inch thickness.

With biscuit cutters, cut five 2½-inch circles; five 2-inch circles; and twenty-five 1-inch circles. Let dough rest before rerolling. Mix egg white and 1 tablespoon *water*.

To assemble each bear, place *one* 2½-inch circle (body) on a baking sheet. Brush edges of *one* 2-inch circle (head) with egg-white mixture; join to body. Brush *four* 1-inch circles (arms and legs) with egg-white mixture; join to body.

Cut *one* 1-inch circle in half (ears). Brush flat side; join to head. Repeat with remaining dough.

Cover assembled bears and let rise in a warm place till nearly double (about 20 minutes). Bake in a 375° oven for 10 to 15 minutes. Brush with Sugar Glaze. Decorate with dried fruit and nuts, if desired. Brush glaze over decorated areas. Makes 10.

Sugar Glaze: Stir together 2 cups sifted *powdered sugar,* ¼ cup *hot water,* and 1 teaspoon *margarine or butter.*

Spritz

Pictured on page 61.

3½ cups all-purpose flour
1 teaspoon baking powder
1½ cups margarine *or* butter

1 cup sugar
1 egg
1 teaspoon vanilla
½ teaspoon almond extract
Food coloring (optional)
Colored sugars *or* decorative candies (optional)

Stir together flour and baking powder. In a large mixer bowl beat margarine or butter till softened. Add sugar and beat till fluffy. Add egg, vanilla, and almond extract; beat well. Gradually add flour mixture; beat till well combined. *Do not chill dough.*

If desired, tint dough with food coloring. Force dough through a cookie press onto an ungreased cookie sheet. Decorate with colored sugars or candies, if desired. Bake in a 400° oven for 7 to 8 minutes or till done. Remove and cool. Makes about 60.

Basic Divinity

2½ cups sugar
 ½ cup light corn syrup
 2 egg whites
 1 teaspoon vanilla
 1 *or* 2 drops desired food
     coloring (optional)
 ½ cup chopped nuts
     (optional)

In a heavy 2-quart saucepan stir together sugar, corn syrup, and ½ cup *water.* Cook over medium-high heat to boiling, stirring constantly to dissolve sugar. Avoid splashing mixture on sides of pan. Clip candy thermometer to pan.

Cook over medium heat, without stirring, till the thermometer registers 260° (hard-ball stage). Mixture should boil at a steady rate over entire surface.

Remove pan from heat; remove thermometer. In a large mixer bowl immediately beat egg whites with a sturdy, freestanding electric mixer on medium speed till stiff peaks form (tips stand straight). *Gradually* pour hot mixture over egg whites, beating on high speed and scraping sides of bowl occasionally. (Add mixture *slowly* to ensure proper blending.)

Add vanilla and food coloring, if desired. Continue beating on high speed just till candy starts to lose its gloss. When beaters are lifted, mixture should fall in a ribbon, but mound on itself and not disappear into remaining mixture. Drop a spoonful of the mixture onto waxed paper. If it stays mounded in a soft shape, it is beaten properly. Immediately stir in nuts, if desired. Quickly drop the remaining mixture from a teaspoon onto a baking sheet lined with waxed paper. If mixture flattens, beat ½ to 1 minute more; check again. If mixture is stiff to spoon and has a rough surface, beat in *hot water,* a few drops at a time, till it is a softer consistency. Store tightly covered. Makes about 40 pieces.

Walnut Caramels

 1 cup chopped walnuts
 1 cup butter *or* margarine
 1 16-ounce package (2¼ cups
     packed) brown sugar
 2 cups light cream
 1 cup light corn syrup
 1 teaspoon vanilla

Line an 8x8x2-inch baking pan with foil. Butter the foil. Sprinkle chopped walnuts on the bottom of the foil-lined pan. Set pan aside.

In a heavy 3-quart saucepan melt the 1 cup butter. Add brown sugar, cream, and corn syrup; mix well. Cook over medium-high heat to boiling, stirring constantly. Avoid splashing the mixture on sides of pan. Carefully clip candy thermometer to side of pan.

Cook over medium heat, stirring frequently, till candy thermometer registers 248° (firm-ball stage). Mixture should boil at a steady rate over entire surface.

Remove pan from heat. Remove candy thermometer. Stir in vanilla. Quickly pour caramel mixture over nuts in prepared pan. When caramel is firm, lift out of pan. Use a buttered knife to cut candy into 1-inch squares. Wrap in clear plastic wrap. Makes 64 pieces or about 2 pounds.

Penuche

1½ cups sugar
 1 cup packed brown sugar
 ⅓ cup light cream
 ⅓ cup milk
 2 tablespoons butter *or*
     margarine
 1 teaspoon vanilla
 ½ cup chopped pecans *or*
     walnuts

Line an 8x4x2-inch or a 9x5x3-inch loaf pan with foil. Butter the foil. Set pan aside.

Butter the sides of a heavy 2-quart saucepan. In the pan combine sugar, brown sugar, cream, and milk. Cook over medium-high heat to boiling, stirring constantly to dissolve sugars. Avoid splashing mixture on sides of pan. Carefully clip candy thermometer to side of pan.

Cook over medium-low heat, stirring frequently, till the thermometer registers 236° (soft-ball stage). Mixture should boil at a steady rate over the entire surface.

Remove pan from heat. Add the 2 tablespoons butter and vanilla, but *do not stir.* Cool mixture, without stirring, to lukewarm (110°). Remove candy thermometer from pan. Beat vigorously with a wooden spoon till penuche is just beginning to thicken; add nuts. Continue beating till penuche becomes very thick and just starts to lose its gloss. Quickly turn penuche into prepared pan. While penuche is warm, score it into 1-inch squares. When candy is firm, use foil to lift it out of pan. Cut candy into squares. Store tightly covered. Makes about 32 pieces or about 1¼ pounds.

Christmastime

A TIME FOR
REMEMBERING

Over the River and Through the Woods

Over the river and through the woods
To Grandmother's house we go.
The horse knows the way to carry the sleigh
Through white and drifted snow.
Over the river and through the woods,
Oh, how the wind does blow.
It stings the toes and bites the nose
As over the ground we go.

Over the river and through the woods
To have a full day of play.
Oh, hear the bells ringing ting-a-ling-ling,
For it is Christmas Day.
Over the river and through the woods,
Trot fast my dapple gray;
Spring o'er the ground just like a hound,
For this is Christmas Day.

Over the river and through the woods
And straight through the barnyard gate.
It seems that we go so dreadfully slow;
It is so hard to wait.
Over the river and through the woods,
Now Grandma's cap I spy.
Hurrah for fun; the pudding's done;
Hurrah for the pumpkin pie.

Tommy's Letters

—J. W. Foley

Appletown, December 1, 1905.

Dear Grandma:

I have often thought of you in the past year but you know how busy boys have to be to keep all the chores done and go to school. We do not get much time to write letters. But the other day I was thinking how kind you had always been to us boys and it was a shame I do not write oftener. So today I sat right down after I came from school to write you a good, long letter and let you know that I often think of you even if I do not write. The ground here is all white with snow which makes us think that it will soon be Christmas again. I suppose you do not care so much for Christmas now as you did when you were a little girl. Mamma says that after folks grow up they do not care so much for it except to make the boys and girls happy by giving them something that they want. It must be awful nice to send a sled or a pair of skates or a tool chest to a boy on Christmas day and think how happy he is. If all of us did that what a bright world it would be. I suppose though that when folks grow up they have so very many things to think about they forget to send things, when they mean to send them all the time but it slips their mind. It isn't that they can't afford it or don't want to but they don't just happen to think about it until it's Christmas day and then it is too late. And then they must feel awful sorry to think how happy it would have made some little boy if they had sent something but they didn't.

I have an idea Eddie Brooks' Grandma is going to send him a sled for Christmas. I don't know what makes me think so, but it seems to me I heard it somewhere. I guess I can make my old one do for another year. One of the runners is broke but I think I can get it fixed. It won't be very safe though.

Dear Grandma, I hope you are having a good winter and your rheumatism don't bother you very much. I often wish I was there to carry out ashes for you and do the heavy work but I have to go to school so I will grow up and be a credit to you all. You know I am named after Grandpa, which makes me all the more anxious to grow up well.

With much love from us all,

Your affectionate grandson,
Tommy

Appletown, December 1, 1905.

Dear Uncle Bill:

I guess you will be surprised when you get this letter because you don't expect any from me but I was writing to Grandma today and I thought I would write to all of our folks and let them know how I am getting along. You know boys don't write very much because they write compositions in school and that takes about all the time they have got to spare for writing. But we ought to write to our relatives once in a while because we are apt to grow up and go away and then the family will be all broke up and scattered. I know you are a bachelor and haven't got any boys to call your own and that maybe it will interest you to know that I'm getting along very well in school because I am your nephew on my mother's side.

It don't seem like over a year since you sent me my pair of skates for Christmas, does it? I wonder if you have changed very much. I have, a good deal. I am tall and my feet are bigger and the skates you sent me are hardly big enough for me now but I guess I can make them do through the winter. One of the straps is wore out but I guess I can have it fixed so it will do. It is quite dangerous to skate with old straps on, though. One of the boys slipped last week and nearly went into an air hole. His skates were too small and one of the straps broke and let him slide.

We ought to be glad of what we have, though, and not expect new skates every year when we are growing so fast.

I suppose you are too busy to think much about Christmas. I enclose you a copy of a letter I wrote to Santa Claus telling what I want. Of course I know all about who Santa Claus is, but I only send it to show you how well I am getting along in writing and spelling. I think Grandmamma is apt to send me the sled and Papa said if I would be a good boy he would get me the tool chest. So that only leaves the skates and if I don't get a new pair the old ones will do.

I hope you are having good health. I wish I could be where I could help you sometimes in your office, cleaning out the wastebasket and doing the sweeping which I would be only too glad to do if we both lived in the same town. We all send our best love to you.

Your affectionate nephew,
Tommy

Appletown, December 1, 1905.

Dear Aunt Lizzie:

Maybe you have almost forgotten about your little nephew Tommy away out here and so I thought I would drop you a few lines to let you know I am well and getting along fine and hope you are the same. I do not write letters very often because you know how it is with boys. They cannot think of many things to say and are apt to make a good many blots if they write with ink. I just happened to think that maybe I had never written to thank you for those splendid books you sent me for last Christmas and as Christmas will soon be here again I do not want to get too far behind. They were splendid books and I have read them all over and over again. I do not know of anything a boy likes better than books. It improves the mind and keeps them out of mischief and when we grow up to be men we can look back and see how the good books we got for Christmas helped to make us better. Nobody ever regrets sending a boy good books for Christmas, don't you think so?

One of the books you sent me had a sequel. It was the Red Ranger or the Mystery of the Indian Scout. The sequel is the Lost Trail or the Lives of the Gold-Hunters. We do not have it in the bookstore here. I am awful anxious to know if the Red Ranger finds the Lost Trail or not. Have you ever read the sequel? If you have I wish you would write and tell me if he finds the lost trail. I have lent the Red Ranger to some of the boys and they will all appreciate very much if you will let us know.

If you know any good books for boys I wish you would write down their names and send them to me.

You know two or three good books will last nearly all winter. Some parts you can read over and over again where there is a lot of excitement until they are nearly worn out. The Red Ranger was that kind and the sequel would probably be almost as good.

It is too bad we are so far away from each other. Sometimes I think how much I could help you and Uncle Jerry not having any boys of your own it would be extremely valuable to you. By chopping wood and filling the woodbox and otherwise doing chores. I could run in on the way from school and see if I couldn't do some chores for you.

I hope you and Uncle Jerry will have a Merry Christmas.

Your affectionate nephew,
Tommy

P.S.—We all send love. The Red Ranger is by the author of the Desert Chief or the Capture of the White Princess.

Tommy

There's no place like home for the holidays!

On Going Home for Christmas

He little knew the sorrow that was in his vacant chair;
He never guessed they'd miss him, or he'd surely have been there;
He couldn't see his mother or the lump that filled her throat,
Or the tears that started falling as she read his hasty note;
And he couldn't see his father, sitting sorrowful and dumb,
Or he never would have written that he thought he
    couldn't come.

He little knew the gladness that his presence would have made,
And the joy it would have given, or he never would have stayed.
He didn't know how hungry had the little mother grown
Once again to see her baby and to claim him for her own.
He didn't guess the meaning of his visit Christmas Day
Or he never would have written that he couldn't get away.

He couldn't see the fading of the cheeks that once were pink,
And the silver in the tresses; and he didn't stop to think
How the years are passing swiftly, and next Christmas it might be
There would be no home to visit and no mother dear to see.
He didn't think about it—I'll not say he didn't care.
He was heedless and forgetful or he'd surely have been there.

Are you going home for Christmas? Have you written you'll
    be there?
Going home to kiss the mother and to show her that you care?
Going home to greet the father in a way to make him glad?
If you're not I hope there'll never come a time you'll
    wish you had.
Just sit down and write a letter—it will make their heart
    strings hum
With a tune of perfect gladness—if you'll tell them that
    you'll come.

—Edgar A. Guest

Heavenly Christmas Ornaments

Create a fantasy all your own
with these beautiful clay ornaments.
Whether they adorn a tree,
evergreens on a mantel, or extra-special
packages, these delicately detailed
maidens, geese, and lambs will be
treasured for years to come.
Follow our instructions for the goose,
kneeling lamb, and girl with
an apron full of hearts.
Then use the same techniques to
craft other trims of your own design.

Clay Ornaments

Shown on pages 74–75.

MATERIALS
Flour, salt, and water (clay)
Paste food coloring (available at
  cake decorating stores)
White acrylic paint
Garlic press; miniature heart and
  flower cutters (available at
  miniatures shops)
Bugle beads (eyes); paraffin
Cookie sheet; plastic bags;
  knives; plastic wrap; foil;
  paper clips; side cutters; straw;
  spatula; and pinking shears

INSTRUCTIONS
Clay (for 6–8 ornaments)
  Mix 1 cup *each* of salt and water,
and 2 cups of flour. Add extra water or flour to make the clay stiff.
  Mix food coloring into *natural-
color* clay to achieve desired
shades. (Mix pink and brown for
flesh color.) Use white paint for
white (or leave clay natural).
Store in plastic bags.
  When rolling clay for flat
shapes, roll ⅛ inch thick.

Lamb
  Make white body, pink ears, assorted color(s) for bow or flowers.

  BODY: Break off a piece of
clay the size of a baby-food jar lid.
Roll into a ball, then into a teardrop shape 1 inch in diameter at
widest point and 3¼ inches long
(narrow end becomes neck). Turn
up narrow end for neck. Set aside.
(The back of the body should lie
flat on the surface.)

HEAD: Break off a piece of
clay the size of a quarter; roll into
a ball. Form nose at one end of
ball, pulling out clay about ⅜ inch;
place on neck of lamb body. Push
two black bugle beads into head
for eyes. Using a knife, pierce Y
shape to define nose.

  EARS: Roll out two teardrop
shapes about ½ inch long (⅜ inch
wide at widest point). Flatten
slightly. Dampen the sides of the
head and press ears in place.

  LEGS: For hind leg, roll out a
coil, 1¾ inches long, leaving one
end larger (about ¾ inch in diameter). Press large end to back of
body; turn narrow end toward
front of lamb.
  For front legs, roll out a ⅜-inch-
diameter coil, 3 inches long; cut in
half. Press foreleg atop back leg
(position the foreleg to the right

of the back leg). Bend legs toward
hind leg.

  TAIL: Press on small oval.

  FLEECE: Using a garlic press,
squeeze out clay ⅛ inch long at a
time; cut off. Moisten the head
slightly; lightly press cut clay
around face. Repeat for body (see
photograph for placement).
  Cut a paper clip in half, using
side cutters. Insert half of paper
clip into body back for hanging.

  LAMB TRIMS: Roll out colored clay for flowers. Cut out with
a miniature cutter; position
around neck. Or, cut a ¼-inch-
wide clay strip; tie into bow.

  FINISHING: Using a spatula,
lift finished ornament onto a foil-
lined cookie sheet. Bake in a 325°
oven for several hours, until hard.
  Melt paraffin in a double boiler; dip ornament into paraffin.

Goose
  Use white clay for body, yellow
for beak and feet, assorted colors for flowers or ribbons.

  BODY: Break off a piece of the
clay and roll into a ball 1½ inches
in diameter. Roll one end, elon-
gating it 2 inches for neck. Pinch
opposite end to form tail.

  NECK AND HEAD: Turn up
elongated end to form neck and
head; poke a hole into elongated
end for beak insertion. Roll small
oval from yellow for beak. Insert
into hole; pinch beak to flatten.
Insert bead eye.

FEET: Roll out two small ovals for the feet, leaving bottom ends of ovals wider for feet; turn up wide ends to form the feet. Press in place.

WING: Roll out a pointed oval for wing; flatten and score one side for feather detail. Press onto body. Insert paper-clip hanger.

GOOSE TRIMS: Make flowers or ribbon streamers as directed for lamb. Fashion ribbon into a bow, or hang ribbons from beak.

FINISHING: Finish as directed above for lamb.

Girl with apron full of hearts

Mix clay as follows: white for apron and feet, peach for dress, flesh for face and hands, pink for cheeks, yellow for hair, blue for hair bow, and assorted colors for the hearts.

DRESS: Roll out peach clay; cut a 3x8-inch rectangle (skirt) and a 1-inch square (bodice).

Place bodice on work surface. To gather dress, push clay into folds by lifting the right side, gathering from right to left. Pinch away excess clay at top of skirt to fit bodice. Press skirt to bodice.

Cover dress with plastic wrap to prevent drying.

APRON: Roll out white clay; cut a 2x4-inch rectangle (apron skirt) and a ¾x1-inch piece (bib) using pinking shears.

Press bib to bodice. Gather 2x4-inch rectangle and press to bib. Score along top edge to simulate gathers. Fold up apron along bottom edge so it will hold hearts.

Using pinking shears, cut an oval from white clay to measure 2 inches long and ½ inch wide at the widest part (apron straps). Cut oval in half lengthwise. Gather straight edge; press to bib front and bodice back.

ARMS: Using peach clay, roll out a 3½-inch-long, ¼-inch-diameter coil; cut in half. Using a pencil, poke a hole in one end of each arm (as for goose head/beak assembly). Round off and smooth other ends for shoulders.

Roll two ovals from flesh-color clay for hands. Moisten holes in arms; press hands into holes.

Press shoulder ends to sides of bodice. Bend arms at the elbows, placing hands at sides of apron.

HEAD: Roll flesh-color clay into an oval about the size of a large olive. Press a small piece of yellow clay onto top of dress; place head on this piece.

Insert bugle beads for eyes. Cut a tiny ball of pink clay in half for the cheeks; roll each half into balls and press onto face. Use a straw to press a grin on face.

HAIR: Using a garlic press, squeeze out about 3- to 4-inch lengths of yellow clay. Press lightly on top of head, twirling and winding lengths into desired hair style.

Insert hook into top of head (see instructions from lamb to make hook). Cut out a ⅛-inch-wide strip from blue clay. Fashion into a bow; press onto hair.

HEARTS: Roll out clay in assorted colors. Using a miniature cutter, cut out enough to fill apron. Press hearts onto apron. Press one heart onto bib.

FEET: From white clay, roll a 4-inch-long, ¼-inch-diameter coil. Cut in half; turn ends up and flatten tips of feet to widen. Press together. Lift bottom of dress; place legs under dress, using a spatula. Press dress to legs.

FINISHING: Finish as directed for lamb ornament.

Victorian Cross-Stitched Stocking

Using ribbons, lace, and sparkling beads, you can personalize this cross-stitched design for your favorite youngster this Christmas.

MATERIALS

⅓ yard *each* of hardanger (or 11-count Aida cloth), fleece, peach cotton fabric (backing), and ecru fabric (lining)

DMC embroidery floss in colors noted under color key, *page 81*

DMC gold metallic thread

1 package of gold crystal beads

1⅔ yards of ¼-inch-wide ecru lace (piping)

½ yard of 1¾-inch-wide pregathered ecru lace trim for the cuff

1 yard of ⅛-inch-wide peach satin ribbon

14 inches of ⅛-inch-wide pink satin ribbon

12 inches of ⅛-inch-wide pink lace

6 inches *each* of ⅝-inch-wide and ½-inch-wide ecru lace

Embroidery hoop and needle

Felt-tip markers

Graph paper

Water-erasable marking pen

INSTRUCTIONS

Charting the pattern

To make a full-color pattern for stocking and cuff, use marking pens to transfer charts on *pages 80 and 81* to graph paper, substituting Xs for the symbols. Chart a name on the cuff, using the letters shown on the chart for inspiration or substituting other alphabets.

Preparing the materials

The stocking body measures approximately 9x15 inches. The cuff strip, excluding lace trim, is 4x14½ inches. Allow ½ inch for the seams and enough fabric around both pieces of the stocking to allow you to place the fabric in a hoop while stitching.

Note: The cross-stitched portion of the stocking will have 5½ inches of *plain* fabric above it. Be especially careful to allow for this before beginning to stitch.

The cross-stitched portion of the cuff is 4x7¼ inches and should be worked on the left-hand side of the cuff strip, allowing an additional 7¼ inches on the right side for the back of the cuff. Be sure to allow for seams.

Using masking tape, tape the raw edges of the fabric to prevent threads from raveling. Separate the embroidery floss and use two strands for working cross-stitches. Separate the metallic thread and use two strands for stitching.

Keep a record of the floss color numbers in case you need to purchase additional amounts. It's best, though, to be sure you've purchased enough floss before you begin, as dye lots may differ slightly.

Stitching the piece

Work stitches over two threads of fabric. Sew beads in place as marked on diagram.

Lace ⅛-inch-wide ribbons beneath the gold stitches (noted by shaded areas on the diagram) in the following order: pink, peach, then pink.

Sew ⅛-inch-wide pink lace in place as indicated by A on the diagram. Use gold running stitches to sew ⅝-inch-wide and ½-inch-wide ecru lace atop pink lace (B and C on diagram).

Sew beads or work peach French knots atop the ecru lace to anchor it in place (see the photograph for reference).

Remove the tape. Press the stitchery, using a warm iron.

Assembling the stocking

Using the marking pen, draw the cuff pattern onto stitched fabric to measure 4x14½ inches. Add a ½-inch seam allowance.

continued

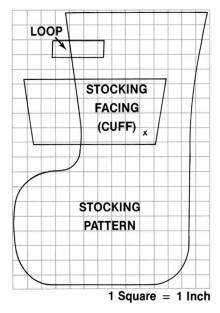

LOOP

STOCKING FACING (CUFF) x

STOCKING PATTERN

1 Square = 1 Inch

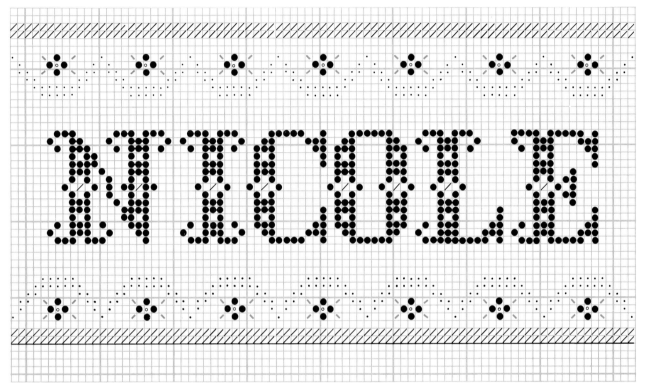

1 Square = 1 Cross-Stitch

Draw stocking pattern onto the stitched fabric, using diagram as a guide. *Note:* You must count fabric threads to establish the stocking perimeter. Add 5 inches to stocking top. Add seams.

Zigzag-stitch along the cutting line *before* cutting out pattern pieces. This will prevent fabric from raveling.

Using the stocking front as a pattern, cut two each from fleece and lining, and one from backing. Using cuff as a pattern, cut one *each* from fleece and lining fabrics.

STOCKING: Stitch the fleece pieces to wrong side of stocking front and back; trim fleece.

Stitch lining pieces together, right sides facing, leaving top open. Trim seams; clip curves.

Sew ¼-inch-wide ecru trim on seam line of stocking front. Sew front to back, right sides facing, leaving top edge open. Clip the curves; turn and press.

CUFF: Sew fleece to wrong side of cuff. Fold cuff in half widthwise, right sides facing, and sew cuff seam. Repeat for the lining, omitting fleece. Sew ¼-inch-wide ecru trim to top of cuff.

With right sides together, slip cuff over lining and sew bottom edges together. Trim seam, turn, and press.

JOINING STOCKING AND CUFF: Insert the cuff into stocking, with the *right* side of cuff facing *wrong* side of stocking top, and matching cuff seam to the left side seam of the stocking.

Stitch the cuff to the stocking top. *Do not sew backing fabric into seam.* Trim seam.

Turn under seam on cuff lining; sew to seam of cuff top and stocking; press.

Turn the cuff to outside of stocking. Sew 1¾-inch-wide lace to the cuff edge.

Weave ⅛-inch-wide peach ribbon through lace (or sew to top edge of lace) and tack a bow to the side. Add loop for hanging.

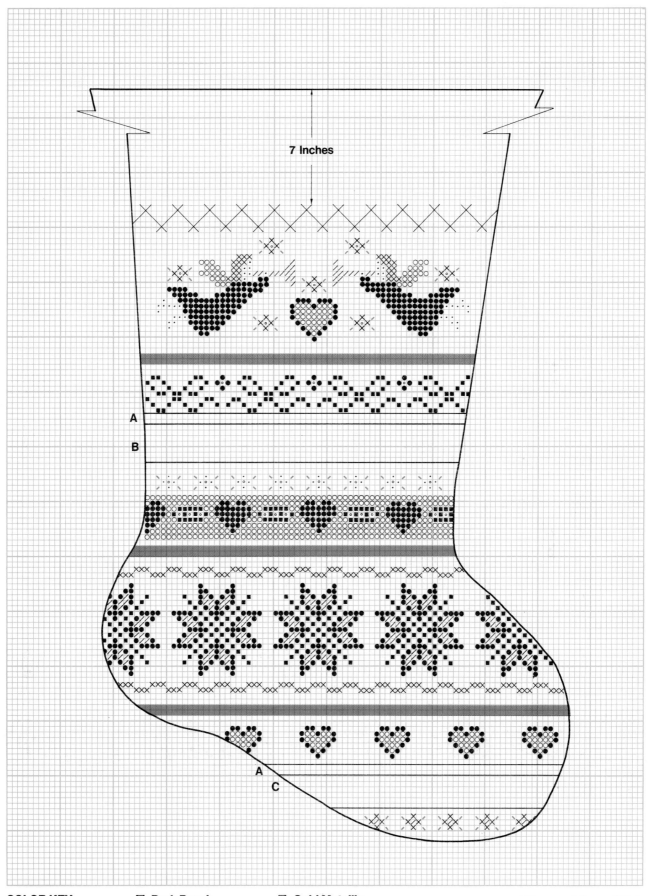

COLOR KEY

⬣ **Rose**	⊠ **Dark Peach**	⬚ **Gold Metallic**
▩ **Green**	⊡ **Light Peach**	⬚ **Green Half Cross-Stitches**
	⬭ **Pink**	⊙ **Gold Beads**

1 Square=1 Cross-Stitch

Traditional Patchwork Nativity

Use the traditional art of patchwork to craft these
delightful figures, piecing them by hand or machine.
Instructions begin on page 84.

Patchwork Nativity

Shown on pages 82–83.

Figures are 12 inches tall.

MATERIALS
¾ yard of muslin
Fabric scraps (see individual instructions)
Tapestry wool (brown, light brown, and black)
Assorted embroidery flosses
Scraps of lace and ribbon for Mary and Infant
Gray and brown felt scraps
Polyester fiberfill
Twigs for staff and cradle
Glue; powdered rouge
Gold cardboard, trim (halo)
Black beads (animal eyes)

INSTRUCTIONS
Enlarge patterns onto paper. A ¼-inch seam is included, unless otherwise stated. For each figure, cut one front and one back from muslin. All other fabric pieces are patched onto muslin fronts and backs. Cut arms from muslin.

For Mary
Cut out paper patterns. Make separate patterns for the eight skirt sections. Add ⅛-inch seams to all inside edges of skirt sections (indicated by Xs on pattern).

FRONT: Cut bodice from beige fabric, making it slightly larger than the area it covers. Baste in place. Cut skirt sections from four prints. Seam two parts (A-1 and A-2) of each skirt section together using ⅛-inch seams; baste section A to muslin front.

With right sides facing and using ⅛-inch seams, sew section B to A, sewing through muslin. Fold B

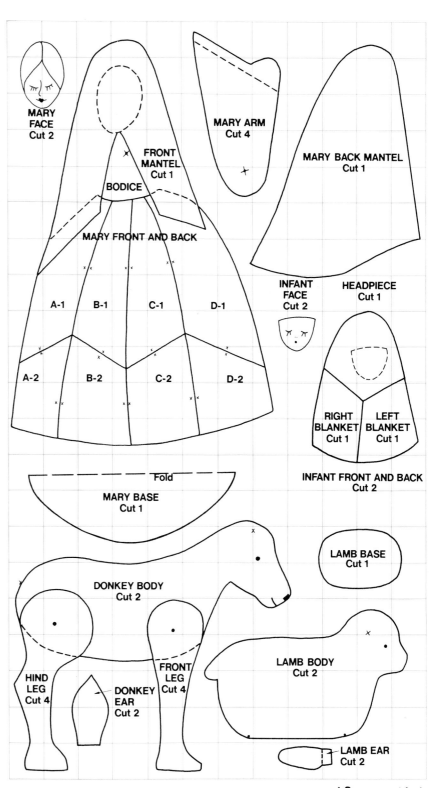

1 Square = 1 Inch

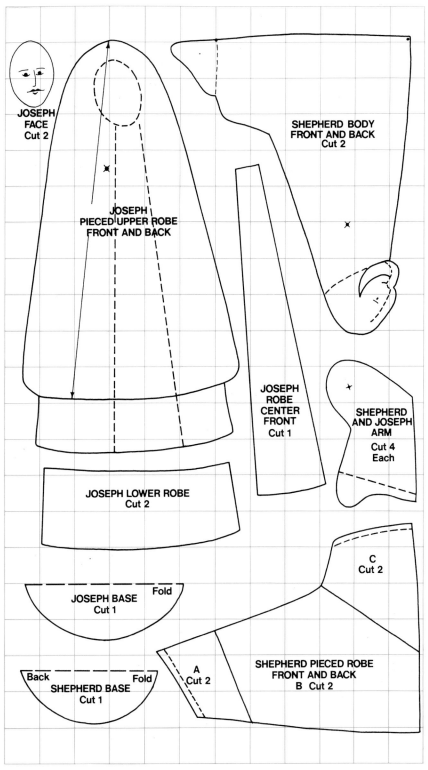

to front; press. Sew section C to B in same manner. Repeat for section D. Baste bottom edge of skirt to muslin. Trim waist with ribbon. Work featherstitches on skirt.

MANTLE: Cut mantle from blue fabric. Stay-stitch ⅛ inch from inside curve. Place atop muslin; baste outside edges. Turn under inside edges; blindstitch.

FACE: Transfer pattern to muslin. Embroider features, using a single strand of floss. Stay-stitch around face outline. Cut out ¼ inch from stitching; appliqué.

HAIR: With one strand of light brown wool, embroider straight stitches for hair. Work French knots at side of face. Color cheeks with rouge. Frame hair with lace.

ARMS: Use the arm pattern for sleeve pattern, eliminating hand. Cut four sleeves from a fifth print fabric. For each arm, turn under straight edge ¼ inch; topstitch to muslin arm along dashed line indicated on pattern. Baste sleeve to arm. Sew one arm together, right sides facing, leaving opening. Clip curves, turn, stuff, and sew opening closed. Repeat for other arm.

BACK: Patch the back in the same manner as directed above, reversing direction on skirt pieces. Exclude bodice section and use the pattern for back mantle. Baste mantle in place, turn under bottom edge, and sew to skirt.

ASSEMBLY: Sew front to back, right sides facing, leaving bottom open. Clip curves; turn. Baste under ¼ inch on bottom edge; stuff.

continued

Draw base pattern onto blue fabric. Sew along this line; cut base ¼ inch from stay stitching. Baste under raw edge. Sew base to bottom of figure; remove basting. Attach arms to body.

HALO: Cut a 3¼-inch-diameter circle from gold cardboard. Glue gold trim around outside edge. Glue to back of head.

For Infant
Piece muslin front as indicated on pattern, using three blue print fabrics. Trim bottom of headpiece with ribbon. Embroider over the seams of the patchwork.

Follow instructions for Mary's face to sew Infant's face. Trim head with lace.

Cut back from blue print; baste to muslin back. Join front and back, right sides facing, leaving opening at bottom. Clip curves, turn, stuff, and sew closed.

Cut a 2¼-inch-diameter gold circle (halo); finish as for Mary.

For Joseph
FRONT AND BACK: Piece enough 1½-inch squares to make a rectangle with 10 rows of six squares each.

Cut the upper robe front from pieced fabric. Baste outside edges to muslin front. Using black thread, quilt an X in every other square. Cut the upper robe back from solid fabric. Baste in place.

Cut bottom robe piece from dark blue print; sew top edge of this piece to bottom edge of top robe. Baste remaining edges to muslin; repeat for back.

Cut out center front panel from solid blue fabric; press under ¼ inch on each side. Blindstitch to dashed lines of pattern.

FACE: Follow instructions for Mary's face. Straight-stitch beard using black tapestry wool.

ASSEMBLY: *For arms,* work as for Mary. *For headpiece,* cut a 6½x13-inch blue print rectangle. Tack in place; tie cord around head. Glue twig staff to hand.

For shepherd
FRONT AND BACK: Piece front and back muslin pieces, using burlap and pumpkin-color fabric. Turn under top edge of pieced front and back to form neckline; topstitch. Turn under raw edge of pieced front and back to form bottom edge of robe (indicated by dashed lines on pattern).

With right sides facing, join front and back, beginning and ending at dots.

Finish assembling figure as described for Mary. Work blanket stitches over seams of patched fabric, using brown tapestry wool.

FACE: Embroider features. Use brown tapestry wool and straight stitches to stitch beard.

HEADPIECE: Cut a 10-inch square of burlap in half diagonally. Using one of the triangles, fold under raw edge on longest side. Wrap this edge over head; tack folds of fabric in place. Tie yarn around head to secure headpiece.

For cradle
Cut nine 5-inch-long twigs. Cross two twigs to form an X; tie together at intersection. Repeat with two more twigs (these are the ends of the cradle). Connect the ends with a third twig by gluing the ends of the third twig across the intersection of each end. Glue

two twigs up each side. Fill with excelsior or straw.

For lamb
On double thickness of white nubby fabric, draw around lamb pattern. *Do not add seam allowances.* Sew along the drawn line, leaving bottom edge open. Trim away excess fabric. Clip the curves; turn and stuff.

Baste under raw edge. Attach base as directed for Mary.

Cut ears from gray felt. Fold over flap; sew ears to head.

Sew black bead eyes in place.

For donkey
BODY: Using beige, brown, and dark brown checked wool fabrics, piece two 6x8-inch rectangles. On the wrong side of one rectangle, draw around body pattern. With right sides of pieced rectangles facing, sew along *drawn* line, leaving bottom open. Trim excess fabric, clip curves, and turn. Stuff; sew opening closed.

HEAD: Sew bead eyes in place. With brown floss, outline-stitch a grin; satin-stitch the nose.

Use tapestry wool and Rya knots for mane. Clip loops. Make tassel at end of a length of wool for tail; tack in place.

Cut two ears from brown felt. Fold bottom edges together to cup the ears; stitch to head at X.

LEGS: On a double thickness of fabric, draw around leg pattern. Sew along this drawn line, leaving an opening for turning. Trim excess fabric. Clip curves, turn, and stuff. Sew opening closed.

Make two legs each from beige and checked wool. Attach legs to body at dots indicated on pattern.

Ready for Christmas

"Ready for Christmas," she said with a sigh
As she gave a last touch to the gifts piled high.
Then wearily sat for a moment to read
Till soon, very soon, she was nodding her head.
Then quietly spoke a voice in her dream,
"Ready for Christmas, what do you mean?
Ready for Christmas when only last week
You wouldn't acknowledge your friend on the street?
Ready for Christmas while holding a grudge?
Perhaps you'd better let God be the judge."
She woke with a start and a cry of despair.
"There's so little time and I've still to prepare.
Oh, Father! Forgive me, I see what you mean!
To be ready means more than a house swept clean.
Yes, more than the giving of gifts and a tree.
It's the heart swept clean that He wanted to see,
A heart that is free from bitterness and sin.
So be ready for Christmas—and ready for Him."

Grammy's Crèche

—Elaine St. Johns

The Grammy who started it all was my mother, Adela Rogers St. Johns. It was after I moved to California with my two-year-old daughter, Kristen and six-year-old son, George. We all lived together, along with an aunt and uncle and various friends and relations, in a family compound called *The Hill*.

As Christmas approached, Grammy decided more than one Christmas tree was redundant, so for her house she bought, instead, a sturdy, rustic, peak-roofed shed, charming Mary and Joseph figurines, a small wooden manger, and of course the Royal Infant Himself. The whole was set up on a living room table surrounded with holiday greens and poinsettias. (The Infant hidden snugly out of sight until Christmas Eve.) The children thought the very merry Christmas tree at our house was for "pretty"; but at Grammy's house, where we gathered together on Christmas Eve, and Baby Jesus appeared in the manger, Grammy's crèche, though simple, was the focus of reverence and awe.

Small wonder that Kristen and George started to save from their pocket money to add to Grammy's crèche. On those long-ago Christmas Eves, as we read the Christmas story from the Gospels, the children would present their gifts. One year an exotic Wise Man; another, four tiny shepherds and one too-large sheep; then a blue ceramic donkey, a plump porcelain angel with a rose atop her head. . . .

The children grew up, married and moved away. Grammy's work as a writer led her to move permanently to a hotel in New York. *The Hill* was no more and the crèche went into storage.

Then my granddaughter was born. It was just before Jessica's first Christmas that a large package was delivered to me from the storage warehouse. The card read, "From one grandmother to another." It was Grammy's crèche. And there they were—Mary and Joseph and Jesus, the Wise Man, the big sheep and too-small shepherds, the blue donkey minus one ear, the angel *sans* rose, but what matter? I carefully set the scene on a table in the living room. After all, more than one Christmas tree is redundant!

It was before this manger that Jessica and later her brother Bogart learned the blessed Christmas story and the beloved carols. And then these two began to bring gifts to the stable. An early offering was a tiny gift-wrapped package of peanuts. Later, with allowances hoarded throughout December, Christmas by Christmas, arrived a variety of angels, several deer, a cow, and more odd sheep. Not quite every beast of the field nor all the great sea monsters gathered before the Holy Family, but there did appear a white horse, an otter, a lion, a handsome orangutan, Jonah's whale and, since Bo found out what Behemoth meant, a hippopotamus.

Grammy's crèche became a neighborhood attraction, with all the children dropping by each year during Christmas week to watch it grow.

Two years ago, Jessica and Bo made an Advent wreath to place at the manger site, and each of the four Sundays before Christmas we ceremoniously lighted a candle and sang carols. This past year they arranged the scene themselves, using my brick fireplace with its raised hearth. Books, stacked to form a series of gentle terraces to the hearth, were covered with a white sheet and cotton snow, sure footing for men and beasts. The fireplace was filled with pine boughs from their yard, and on the hearth itself was the crèche with its familiar, well-loved figures.

On Christmas Eve, as Jessica, now ten, placed the Infant in His manger and her mother, father, Bo and I sang one last "Silent Night," I inwardly thanked my mom for her gift. Not only for the tangible objects themselves but for her gift of wisdom in establishing a tradition that strengthens our family and its sense of continuity. For one day, I know, in the not-too-distant future, I will give my daughter Grammy's crèche: "From one grandmother to another."

Joy to the World

Joy to the world! the Lord has come:
Let earth receive her King.
Let ev'ry heart prepare Him room,
And heav'n and nature sing, and heav'n and nature sing,
And heav'n, and heav'n and nature sing.

Joy to the world! the Savior reigns:
Let men their songs employ,
While fields and floods, rocks, hills and plains
Repeat the sounding joy, repeat the sounding joy,
Repeat, repeat the sounding joy.

He rules the world with truth and grace,
And makes the nations prove
The glories of His righteousness
And wonders of His love, and wonders of His love,
And wonders, wonders of His love.

The Miraculous Staircase

—Arthur Gordon

On that cool December morning in 1878, sunlight lay like an amber rug across the dusty streets and adobe houses of Santa Fe. It glinted on the bright tile roof of the almost completed Chapel of Our Lady of Light and on the nearby windows of the convent school run by the Sisters of Loretto. Inside the convent, the Mother Superior looked up from her packing as a tap came on her door.

"It's *another* carpenter, Reverend Mother," said Sister Francis Louise, her round face apologetic. "I told him that you're leaving right away, that you haven't time to see him, but he says. . . ."

"I know what he says," Mother Magdalene said, going on resolutely with her packing. "That he's heard about our problem with the new chapel. That he's the best carpenter in all of New Mexico. That he can build us a staircase to the choir loft despite the fact that the brilliant architect in Paris who drew the plans failed to leave any space for one. And despite the fact that five master carpenters have already tried and failed. You're quite right, Sister; I don't have time to listen to that story again."

"But he seems such a nice man," said Sister Francis Louise wistfully, "and he's out there with his burro, and. . . ."

"I'm sure," said Mother Magdalene with a smile, "that he's a charming man, and that his burro is a charming donkey. But there's sickness down at the Santo Domingo pueblo, and it may be cholera. Sister Mary Helen and I are the only ones here who've had cholera. So we have to go. And you have to stay and run the school. And that's that!" Then she called, "Manuela!"

A young Indian girl of 12 or 13, black-haired and smiling, came in quietly on moccasined feet. She was a mute. She could hear and understand, but the Sisters had been unable to teach her to speak. The Mother Superior spoke to her gently: "Take my things down to the wagon, child. I'll be right there." And to Sister Francis Louise: "You'd better tell your carpenter friend to come back in two or three weeks. I'll see him then."

"Two or three weeks! Surely you'll be home for Christmas?"

"If it's the Lord's will, Sister. I hope so."

In the street, beyond the waiting wagon, Mother Magdalene could see the carpenter, a bearded man, strongly built and taller than most Mexicans, with dark eyes and a smiling, wind-burned face. Beside him, laden with tools and scraps of lumber, a small gray burro stood patiently. Manuela was stroking its nose, glancing shyly at its owner. "You'd better explain," said the Mother Superior, "that the child can hear him, but she can't speak."

Goodbyes were quick—the best kind when you leave a place you love. Southwest, then, along the dusty trail, the mountains purple with shadow, the Rio Grande a ribbon of green far off to the right. The pace was slow, but Mother Magdalene and Sister Mary Helen amused themselves by singing songs and telling Christmas stories as the sun marched up and down

the sky. And their leathery driver listened and nodded.

Two days of this brought them to Santo Domingo Pueblo, where the sickness was not cholera after all, but measles, almost as deadly in an Indian village. And so they stayed, helping the harassed Father Sebastian, visiting the dark adobe hovels where feverish brown children tossed and fierce Indian dogs showed their teeth.

At night they were bone-weary, but sometimes Mother Magdalene found time to talk to Father Sebastian about her plans for the dedication of the new chapel. It was to be in April; the Archbishop himself would be there. And it might have been dedicated sooner, were it not for this incredible business of a choir loft with no means of access—unless it were a ladder.

"I told the Bishop," said Mother Magdalene, "that it would be a mistake to have the plans drawn in Paris. If something went wrong, what could we do? But he wanted our chapel in Santa Fe patterned after the Sainte Chapelle in Paris, and who am I to argue with Bishop Lamy? So the talented Monsieur Mouly designs a beautiful choir loft high up under the rose window, and no way to get to it."

"Perhaps," sighed Father Sebastian, "he had in mind a heavenly choir. The kind with wings."

"It's not funny," said Mother Magdalene a bit sharply. "I've prayed and prayed, but apparently there's no solution at all. There just isn't room on the chapel floor for the supports such a staircase needs."

The days passed, and with each passing day Christmas drew closer. Twice, horsemen on their way from Santa Fe to Albuquerque brought letters from Sister Francis Louise. All was well at the convent, but Mother Magdalene frowned over certain paragraphs. "The children are getting ready for Christmas," Sister Francis Louise wrote in her first letter. "Our little Manuela and the carpenter have become great friends. It's amazing how much he seems to know about us all. . . ."

And what, thought Mother Magdalene, is the carpenter still doing there?

The second letter also mentioned the carpenter. "Early every morning he comes with another load of lumber, and every night he goes away. When we ask him by what authority he does these things, he smiles and says nothing. We have tried to pay him for his work, but he will accept no pay. . . ."

Work? What work? Mother Magdalene wrinkled up her nose in exasperation. Had that soft-hearted Sister Francis Louise given the man permission to putter around in the new chapel? With firm and disapproving hand, the Mother Superior wrote a note ordering an end to all such unauthorized activities. She gave it to an Indian pottery-maker on his way to Santa Fe.

But that night the first snow fell, so thick and heavy that the Indian turned back. Next day at noon the sun shone again on a world glittering with diamonds. But Mother Magdalene knew

continued

that another snowfall might make it impossible for her to be home for Christmas. By now the sickness at Santo Domingo was subsiding. And so that afternoon they began the long ride back.

The snow did come again, making their slow progress even slower. It was late on Christmas Eve, close to midnight, when the tired horses plodded up to the convent door. But lamps still burned. Manuela flew down the steps, Sister Francis Louise close behind her. And chilled and weary though she was, Mother Magdalene sensed instantly an excitement, an electricity in the air that she could not understand.

Nor did she understand it when they led her, still in her heavy wraps, down the corridor, into the new, as-yet-unused chapel where a few candles burned. "Look, Reverend Mother," breathed Sister Francis Louise. "Look!"

Like a curl of smoke the staircase rose before them, as insubstantial as a dream. Its base was on the chapel floor; its top rested against the choir loft. Nothing else supported it; it seemed to float on air. There were no banisters. Two complete spirals it made, the polished wood gleaming softly in the candlelight. "Thirty-three steps," whispered Sister Francis Louise. "One for each year in the life of Our Lord."

Mother Magdalene moved forward like a woman in a trance. She put her foot on the first step, then the second, then the third. There was not a tremor. She looked down, bewildered, at Manuela's ecstatic, upturned face. "But it's impossible! There wasn't time!"

"He finished yesterday," the Sister said. "He didn't come today. No one has seen him any-where in Santa Fe. He's gone."

"But *who* was he? Don't you even know his *name?*"

The Sister shook her head, but now Manuela pushed forward, nodding emphatically. Her mouth opened; she took a deep, shuddering breath; she made a sound that was like a gasp in the stillness. The nuns stared at her, transfixed. She tried again. This time it was a syllable, followed by another. "Jo-sé." She clutched the Mother Superior's arm and repeated the first word she had ever spoken. "José!"

Sister Francis Louise crossed herself. Mother Magdalene felt her heart contract. José—the Spanish word for Joseph. Joseph the Carpenter. Joseph the Master Woodworker of. . . .

"José!" Manuela's dark eyes were full of tears. "José!"

Silence, then, in the shadowy chapel. No one moved. Far away across the snow-silvered town Mother Magdalene heard a bell tolling midnight. She came down the stairs and took Manuela's hand. She felt uplifted by a great surge of wonder and gratitude and compassion and love. And she knew what it was. It was the spirit of Christmas. And it was upon them all.

Note: With the exception of the banister that was added later, this stairway stands today in Sante Fe just as it did 90 years ago when the chapel was dedicated. It's believed the wood that this staircase was made from is a hard-fir variety—nonexistent in New Mexico. Visitors marvel at the 33 steps that make two complete turns without central support, and at the fact that there are no nails holding the staircase together—only wooden pegs.

And it came to pass in those days, that there went out a decree from Caesar Augustus, that all the world should be taxed. (And this taxing was first made when Cyrenius was governor of Syria.) And all went to be taxed, every one into his own city. And Joseph also went up from Galilee, out of the city of Nazareth, into Judea, unto the city of David, which is called Bethlehem, (because he was of the house and lineage of David), to be taxed with Mary his espoused wife, being great with child. And so it was, that, while they were there, the days were accomplished that she should be delivered. And she brought forth her firstborn son, and wrapped him in swaddling clothes, and laid him in a manger; because there was no room for them in the inn. And there were in the same country shepherds abiding in the field, keeping watch over their flock by night. And, lo, the angel of the Lord came upon them, and the glory of the Lord shown round about them; and they were sore afraid. And the angel said unto them. Fear not: for, Behold, I bring you good tidings of great joy, which shall be to all people. For unto you is born this day in the city of David a Saviour, which is Christ the Lord. And this shall be a sign unto you: Ye shall find the babe wrapped in swaddling clothes, lying in a manger. And suddenly there was with the angel a multitude of the heavenly host praising God, and saying, Glory to God in the highest, and on earth peace, good will toward men. And it came to pass, as the angels were gone away from them into heaven, the shepherds said one to another, Let us now go even unto Bethlehem, and see this thing which is come to pass, which the Lord hath made known unto us. And they came with haste, and found Mary and Joseph, and the babe lying in a manger. And when they had seen it, they made known abroad the saying which was told them concerning this child. And all they that heard it wondered at those things which were told them by the shepherds. But Mary kept all these things, and pondered them in her heart. And the shepherds returned, glorifying and praising God for all the things that they had heard and seen, as it was told unto them."

—*St. Luke 2:1–20*

A Tale for Christmas Evening

Now that you're tired of your toys, Sonny Boy,
    And you're cocking a sleepy eye,
Climb into my lap and I'll tell you a tale
    Of a time that is long gone by.

Over the sea, in a little old town—
    No, your daddy was never there—
A Baby was born on the first Christmas day,
    In a place that was chill and bare.

He had no fire like the one we have here,
    Where His mother could warm His toes,
Not even a roof covered over His head,
    But the stars saw His eyelids close.

Yes, He was poor, but withal was a King,
    As the Wise Men afar had been told;
And they came on their camels to bring Him rare gifts
    Of frankincense, myrrh and gold.

Where is He now? Why He's here in our home,
    But don't look for Him with your eyes,
For he is the Spirit of Love, Sonny Boy,
    And of ev'rything good and wise.

—Lucy Carruth

Two Prayers for Children

On Christmas Morning

Let angels sing a little song
Deep in my heart the whole day long—
Let me be satisfied and glad
With every gift that I have had,
And let me think the kindly things
That are as gay as birds on wings.
In everything I say or do, dear Jesus
Let me be like you! Amen.

On Christmas Night

Let candlelight upon the tree
My family have made for me,
Be soft with happiness and love
Reflected from the sky above.
Oh, let me, as I go to sleep,
Feel little dreams about me creep,
And let me say this evening prayer
For all the children, everywhere!
                    Amen

Norman Rockwell

Christmas Magic
Love Lives Through the Eyes of a Child

—by Charlene Gaynor

nce again, the Christmas miracle had happened. I had lived through the rush of frantic shoppers jousting for space at the sale tables. 'Tis the season to be jolly. "Hold that thought," I muttered, vowing as usual that next year would be different.

The combination of crowded stores and overpriced merchandise had pushed my Christmas spirit to the limit. Even worse, the drone of crying children and frenzied parents was progressing from a mild buzzing to a full-blown explosion in the back of my head.

With the useless trinket for the aunt who has everything finally tucked into my bag, only one ceremony remained. I watched impatiently as the wide-eyed child made her way to Santa's throne. She was oblivious to the camera in front of the makeshift wonderland and to the elves eagerly waiting to preserve her visit on film for the bargain price of $8 a shot.

The little girl climbed gingerly into Santa's lap, as had countless children in countless wonderlands before her. He smiled into her eyes and she smiled back. I looked on from a distance and saw something indefinable pass between them.

The smiles progressed to polite conversation. With his arm tightly around her, Santa talked almost in whispers and only to her. He talked about her dimples and her braids and her baby brother. Soon, they were engaged in an intimate exchange. The child poured out the innermost desires of her four-year-old heart. Santa nodded intently.

Oblivious now to the absurdity of the picture-taking elves, I watched the timeless ritual unfold before me. But this time, the scene was somehow different. The child I was watching was mine.

The two continued in deep conversation until all the whispered secrets had been shared. Then, the old man hugged my little girl tightly. "Santa loves you very much," he said. She beamed and squeezed him back.

Quite unexpectedly, I started to cry.

The old man looked past the cameras and lights and glimpsed a toddler standing beside his mother, me, clutching her hand in fear and wonderment. He rose from his throne, my girl by his side, and came forward.

Santa took the hand of my little boy and touched his head in a simple gesture. "Merry Christmas, little one," he said. "And a blessed Christmas to you, mom."

I looked up and was startled. He was very old—too old to fit the role of the storybook Santa, robust, healthy and smooth-skinned. Behind the cotton beard and furry hat, his face was thick and wrinkled. His yellowed eyes didn't twinkle. And his hand shook a little as he handed my son a Christmas coloring book.

Just for a moment, our eyes met. Then, Santa turned and walked feebly back to his throne. Another little girl climbed into his lap. His eyes smiled and the silent magic happened. Soon, they were completely absorbed.

As we walked away from the wooden wonderland, my daughter kept turning around, straining to get just one more look. "Santa is so special," she sighed. She took my hand as the three of us made our way across the crowded mall.

Then, just once in spite of myself, I looked back, too.

Merry Christmas

This Would I Keep

This would I keep forever in my heart
Among the things the ruthless years may leave:
The glad excitement, wonder, and delight
Of Christmas Eve;

This would I hold untarnished through the years,
Although the roads I take may lead me far:
The radiant molten glory of the light
From one white star.

And oh, to keep the breathlessness, the thrill,
The heart's swift running out to meet surprise,
Never to lose entirely the light
Of childhood from my eyes;

Never to lose the Christmas morning joy,
And never the quick bright eagerness to give—
God, someway let my spirit keep the shine
Of Christmas while I live.

—Grace Noll Crowell

It is good to be children sometimes, and never
better than at Christmas, when its mighty Founder
was a child Himself.

—Charles Dickens

Mincemeat has filled the winter air with its spicy scent
for centuries. In fact, it virtually has come to taste like
Christmas to many. So whether you're trying
mincemeat as a first-timer or a connoisseur, you're
going to love what Christmas tastes like this year.

A Christmas Tradition: Mincemeat

Traditional Mincemeat

1½ pounds lean beef rump, neck, *or* chuck, cubed
½ pound suet, finely chopped
4 pounds firm, tart apples, peeled, cored, and finely chopped
3 cups cider
2 cups sugar
1 15-ounce package dark raisins
1 15-ounce package golden raisins
1 10-ounce package currants
⅔ cup diced citron
⅔ cup diced candied fruit
½ cup molasses
4 teaspoons ground cinnamon
2 teaspoons salt
1½ teaspoons ground nutmeg
1½ teaspoons ground mace
2 cups sherry
1 cup brandy

In a medium saucepan cover beef with water. Boil 1½ hours or till tender. Cool.

In a blender container or food processor finely chop meat. In a kettle combine chopped meat, suet, apples, cider, sugar, raisins, currants, citron, candied fruit, molasses, cinnamon, salt, nutmeg, mace, and ¼ teaspoon *pepper*.

Bring mixture to boiling, stirring occasionally. Stir in the sherry and the brandy. Simmer for 30 minutes, stirring often. (If the mixture becomes too thick, stir in more cider.)

To freeze: Place 1- or 2-cup portions in moisture- and vaporproof containers. Seal, label, and freeze.
To can: Pack the hot mixture into hot, clean pint jars, leaving ½-inch headspace. Adjust lids. Process in pressure canner at 10 pounds of pressure for 20 minutes. Makes 10 pints.

Mincemeat: A Flavorful History

As an early English writer once said, "He that discovered the new star in Cassiopeia deserves not half so much to be remembered as he that first married meat and raisins."

The origins of mincemeat—a rich mixture of minced meat, suet, fruit, and spices—are obscure. But the mince pie may have been born during the time of the Crusades. Preparing for a holiday feast, a daring cook may have added exotic spices brought back from the East to a mixture of minced meat, dried fruits, lemon peel, juice, and sweetening, then baked the mixture in a rectangular "coffin," or crust.

The Christmas association of this new dish was strengthened by lore that likened the shape of the pie to Christ's manger and the spices to the offerings of the wise men. It became the custom to eat one pie a day between Christmas and Twelfth Night, as each was thought to bring good luck.

Mince pies became as popular in the New World as they had been in England.

The first cookbook produced in America, written in 1796, offered a simple recipe for mince pie. Adaptability may have been the key to mincemeat's longevity. Ingredients were easily varied as the time and place required.

During the 1870s, great gains were made in the field of food preservation. Condensed mincemeat continues to be a boon for cooks, but delicious old-fashioned versions of this Christmas classic are easy to make from scratch.

Mincemeat Braid

Pictured on page 102.

1 cup Traditional *or* Fruit
   Mincemeat (see recipes,
   pages 103 and 107)
½ cup chopped peeled apple
⅓ cup chopped walnuts
3 to 3¾ cups all-purpose
   flour
1 package active dry yeast
1 cup milk
¼ cup sugar
¼ sup shortening
1 egg
1 tablespoon finely shredded
   lemon peel

For filling, combine mincemeat, apple, and nuts. Set aside.

Mix *1½ cups* of the flour and yeast. Heat milk, sugar, shortening, and ½ teaspoon *salt* just till warm (115° to 120°) and shortening almost melts, stirring constantly. Add to flour mixture. Add egg and lemon peel. Beat with an electric mixer on low speed for 30 seconds, scraping bowl. Beat on high speed for 3 minutes. Stir in as much remaining flour as you can.

Turn out onto a floured surface. Knead in enough remaining flour to make a soft dough that is smooth and elastic (3 to 5 minutes total). Shape into a ball. Place in a greased bowl, turning once. Cover; let rise in a warm place till double (about 45 minutes).

Punch down. Divide in half. Cover; let rest 10 minutes. Divide each half into 3 portions. Roll 1 portion into a 12x4-inch rectangle. Spread *3 tablespoons* filling down center. Bring long sides together; seal edge. Place on greased baking sheet. Repeat with 2 more portions of dough and filling. Braid 3 filled portions together. Seal ends. Repeat with remaining dough and filling. Cover and let rise till nearly double (about 45 minutes). Bake in a 350° oven for 25 to 30 minutes. Cool on a wire rack. Makes 2.

Tiny Mince Tarts

½ cup margarine *or* butter,
   softened
1 3-ounce package cream
   cheese, softened
1 cup all-purpose flour
1¼ cups Traditional *or* Fruit
   Mincemeat (see recipes,
   pages 103 and 107)
½ cup chopped walnuts
1 tablespoon finely shredded
   orange peel
2 teaspoons finely shredded
   lemon peel

Beat together margarine or butter and cream cheese. Stir in flour. If necessary, cover and chill about 1 hour or till easy to handle. Shape into 1-inch balls. Press onto bottoms and up sides of ungreased 1¾-inch muffin cups.

For filling, combine mincemeat, nuts, and orange and lemon peel. Place *1 rounded teaspoon* filling in *each* cup. Bake in a 350° oven for 25 to 30 minutes or till done. Cool slightly in pans. Remove; cool on wire rack. Makes 24.

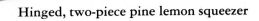

Hinged, two-piece pine lemon squeezer

Christmas Strudel

Pictured on page 104.

    5 sheets frozen phyllo dough
        (17x12-inch rectangles),
        thawed
    ⅓ cup margarine *or* butter,
        melted
    ⅓ cup fine dry bread crumbs
        Mince-Pear Filling
        Powdered Sugar

Unroll phyllo dough; cover with a damp towel. Remove 1 sheet at a time. Brush with some margarine; sprinkle with some crumbs. Top with a second sheet. Brush with margarine; sprinkle with crumbs. Repeat with remaining phyllo.

Spoon Mince-Pear Filling along 1 long side. Roll up jelly-roll style. Cut in half crosswise. Place on a lightly greased 15x10x1-inch baking pan. Brush with remaining margarine. Bake in a 350° oven for 45 to 50 minutes. Transfer from pan to rack. Cool. Sift sugar over top. Makes 6 to 8 servings.

Mince-Pear Filling: Combine 1 cup coarsely chopped peeled *pear,* ¾ cup *Fruit Mincemeat* (see recipe, page 107), and 1 teaspoon finely shredded *lemon peel.*

Mince Marble Cake

Pictured on page 104.

    2½ cups all-purpose flour
    2½ teaspoons baking powder
    1½ cups sugar
     ¾ cup margarine *or* butter
      2 eggs
    1½ teaspoons vanilla
     ¾ cup apple juice
      1 cup Traditional *or* Fruit
        Mincemeat (see recipes,
        pages 103 and 107)
        Apple Icing

Grease and flour a 10-inch fluted tube pan. Set aside. Combine flour and baking powder. Beat together sugar and margarine till light and fluffy. Add eggs and vanilla; beat till light and fluffy. Add dry ingredients alternately with apple juice. Beat on low speed after each addition. Fold in mincemeat. Pour into prepared pan.

Bake in a 350° oven for 50 to 55 minutes or till done. Cool in pan 10 minutes. Remove from pan. Cool on wire rack. Drizzle with Apple Icing. Serves 12 to 16.

Apple Icing: Combine 1 cup sifted *powdered sugar* and about 1 tablespoon *apple juice.* Add more juice, if needed, to drizzle.

Iron apple peeler

Mincemeat Star Cookies

Pictured on page 104.

      1 cup shortening
     ½ cup margarine *or* butter
      2 cups sugar
      2 eggs
     ¼ milk
      2 teaspoons finely shredded
        orange peel
      1 teaspoon vanilla
    4½ cups all-purpose flour
      1 teaspoon baking soda
      2 cups Traditional *or* Fruit
        Mincemeat (see recipes,
        pages 103 and 107)

For dough, beat shortening and margarine on medium speed about 30 seconds. Add sugar; beat till fluffy. Add eggs, milk, orange peel, and vanilla; beat well.

Combine flour, soda, and ½ teaspoon *salt.* On low speed gradually add flour mixture to shortening mixture, beating well. Divide into quarters. Chill dough 3 hours.

On a floured surface roll 1 portion of dough to ⅛-inch thickness. Cut cookies with a 2½-inch round cookie cutter. Using an hors d'oeuvre cutter, cut a small star from center of *half* the cookies. Place *1 teaspoon* mincemeat on *each* plain cookie. Top with a cutout

Cast-iron raisin seeder

cookie. Press edges to seal.

Place cookies on an ungreased cookie sheet. Bake in a 375° oven for 10 to 12 minutes or till lightly browned. Repeat with remaining dough. Cool on wire racks. Makes 3 dozen cookies.

Cherry-Mincemeat Pie

Pictured on page 102.

    Pastry for two-crust 9-inch pie
1 21-ounce can cherry pie filling
1 cup Traditional Mincemeat (see recipe, page 103)
¼ cup chopped walnuts
¼ cup orange marmalade
2 teaspoons all-purpose flour

Prepare and roll out pastry. Line a 9-inch pie plate with *half* of the pastry. Trim pastry to ½ inch beyond edge of pie plate.

Stir together pie filling, mincemeat, nuts, marmalade, and flour. Transfer to pastry-lined pie plate. Cut remaining pastry into ½-inch-wide strips. Weave strips atop filling to make lattice. Press ends of strips into rim of crust. Fold bottom pastry over lattice strips. Seal and flute. To prevent overbrowning, cover edge with foil.

Bake in a 375° oven for 20 minutes. Remove foil; bake 20 to 25 minutes more. Serve with vanilla ice cream, if desired. Serves 8.

Fruit Mincemeat

1½ pounds firm pears, peeled, cored, and chopped
½ pound firm, tart apples, peeled, cored, and chopped
¾ cup dark raisins
¾ cup golden raisins
¾ cup chopped dried figs
¾ cup chopped dried apricots
¾ cup packed brown sugar
½ cup slivered almonds, toasted
1 tablespoon chopped candied ginger
½ teaspoon ground cinnamon
¼ teaspoon ground mace
¼ teaspoon ground nutmeg
1 tablespoon finely shredded lemon *or* orange peel
⅓ cup lemon *or* orange juice
¼ cup brandy

Combine all ingredients. Bring to boiling, stirring occasionally. Cook 2 minutes more, stirring often. Pack mixture in 1-cup portions and refrigerate for up to 5 days or freeze for up to 4 months.
To can: Pack into hot, clean ½-pint jars, leaving ½-inch headspace. Process in boiling-water bath for 10 minutes (begin timing when water returns to boiling.) Makes 6 or 7 half-pints.

Apple corer

Christmas Morning Brunch

Looking for a comfortable, laid-back way to greet out-of-town kin or to welcome the family on Christmas morning? Treat your guests to this holiday brunch menu that will start out the day in a very merry way.

Cranberry-Pear Braid

Pictured opposite.

  4 cups all-purpose flour
  1 package active dry yeast
1¼ cups milk
  ¼ cup packed brown sugar
  ¼ cup margarine *or* butter
  2 eggs
  3 cups peeled, cored, and
       chopped pears
1½ cups fresh cranberries
  1 cup sugar
  3 tablespoons cornstarch
  ½ cup chopped toasted
       almonds
       Powdered Sugar Icing

In a large mixer bowl combine *1½ cups* of flour and yeast. In a saucepan heat milk, brown sugar, margarine, and ½ teaspoon *salt* just till warm (115° to 120°) and margarine is almost melted, stirring constantly. Add to flour mixture; add eggs. Beat with an electric mixer on low speed for 30 seconds, scraping sides of bowl constantly. Beat on high speed for 3 minutes. Using a spoon, stir in remaining flour to make a soft dough. Shape into a ball. Cover; refrigerate several hours or overnight.

For filling, cook and stir pears, cranberries, and sugar about 10 minutes or till tender. Combine cornstarch and 2 tablespoons *water*. Add to cranberry mixture. Cook and stir for 2 minutes more. Stir in nuts. Cool.

Punch dough down. Divide in half. Return one portion to refrigerator. On a floured surface roll other portion into a 15x12-inch rectangle. Cut dough lengthwise into three 15x4-inch rectangles. Spread about *½ cup filling* down center of *each* rectangle. Bring long sides of each rectangle together and seal. Seal ends. Place filled dough strips, seam sides down and 1 inch apart, on a greased baking sheet. Braid loosely, beginning at middle and working toward ends. Pinch ends together; tuck under. Repeat with remaining dough and filling.

Cover; let rise in a warm place till almost double, about 30 minutes. Bake in a 350° oven for 25 to 30 minutes or till golden. If necessary, cover loosely with foil the last 5 minutes. Cool on wire racks. Drizzle with Powdered Sugar Icing. Makes 2 braids.

Powdered Sugar Icing: Combine 2 cups sifted *powdered sugar,* ½ teaspoon *vanilla,* and enough *milk* for drizzling.

Pork Sausage Ring

Pictured opposite.

  2 eggs
  ½ cup milk
1½ cups crushed saltine
       crackers (42)
  1 cup chopped peeled apple
  ¼ cup chopped onion
  2 pounds bulk pork sausage
       Creamy Scrambled Eggs
       (see recipe, page 110)
       Sautéed Apple Slices
       (optional)

Combine eggs and milk. Stir in crushed crackers, apple, onion, and ¼ teaspoon *pepper.* Add sausage; mix well. Firmly pat mixture into a 6½-cup ring mold. Carefully unmold sausage ring onto a rack in a shallow baking pan. Bake in a 350° oven for 50 minutes. Transfer to a warm platter. Fill center of ring with Creamy Scrambled Eggs. Garnish with the Sautéed Apple Slices, if desired. Serves 12.

Sautéed Apple Slices: Melt 1 tablespoon *margarine or butter.* Core and slice 1 medium *apple.* Cook apple slices in margarine just till tender, turning occasionally.

Continue cooking for 8 to 10 minutes or till the eggs are cooked throughout, but are still moist and glossy. Pile inside Pork Sausage Ring. Makes 12 servings.

Fattigman

Pictured opposite.

6 egg yolks
¼ cup sugar
⅓ cup whipping cream, whipped
1½ cups all-purpose flour
1½ teaspoons ground cardamom
Cooking oil
Powdered sugar *or* sugar

Beat egg yolks about 5 minutes or till thick and lemon colored. Gradually beat in sugar. Fold in whipped cream. Combine flour, cardamom, and ¼ teaspoon *salt.* Fold into egg mixture, a little at a time, to make a soft dough. Cover; chill several hours or overnight.

Divide dough in half. On a floured surface, roll each half into a 12-inch square about ⅛ inch thick. Using a pastry wheel or knife, cut dough into 3x2-inch diamonds. Make a ¾-inch lengthwise slit in center of each diamond. Pull one end of cookie through the slit.

Fry, a few at a time, in deep hot oil (375°) for 40 to 50 seconds or till very light brown, turning once. Drain well. Sprinkle with sugar. Makes about 30.

Creamy Scrambled Eggs

Pictured on page 108.

1½ cups light cream *or* milk
1 8-ounce package cream cheese, softened
2 tablespoons snipped parsley
1¼ teaspoons dried basil, crushed
16 eggs
4 tablespoons margarine *or* butter
Pork Sausage Ring (see recipe, page 109)

In a blender container combine cream, cream cheese, parsley, basil, and ¼ teaspoon *pepper.* Cover and blend till mixed.

In a large bowl beat the eggs just till foamy. Add cream cheese mixture, stirring to combine.

In a 12-inch skillet or two 10-inch skillets melt the margarine over medium heat. Pour the egg mixture into the skillet. Cook, without stirring, till egg mixture begins to set on the bottom and around the edges. Lift and fold partially cooked eggs so uncooked portion flows underneath.

Sunshine Slush

To offer the slush with and without liquor, pour equal amounts of the fruit juice mixture into two 8x8x2-inch baking pans and stir ¾ cup of the liquor into one pan before freezing. Pictured on page 108.

1 cup sugar
2 ripe medium bananas, cut up
2 12-ounce cans (3 cups) unsweetened pineapple juice
1 6-ounce can frozen orange juice concentrate, thawed
1 6-ounce can frozen lemonade concentrate, thawed
2 tablespoons lemon juice
1½ cups rum *or* vodka (optional)
1 28-ounce bottle carbonated water, chilled

In a saucepan combine sugar and 3 cups *water.* Bring to boiling, stirring till sugar is dissolved. Boil gently, uncovered, for 3 minutes. Remove from heat and cool.

Meanwhile, in a blender container combine the cut-up bananas and *half* of the unsweetened pineapple juice. Cover and blend just till smooth.

Stir in cooled sugar mixture. Stir in remaining pineapple juice, orange juice concentrate, lemonade concentrate, and lemon juice. Stir in rum or vodka, if desired.

Transfer fruit juice mixture to a 13x9x2-inch pan or plastic freezer container. Cover with moisture- and vaporproof material. Seal, la-bel, and freeze for at least several hours or as long as 2 months. (If desired, break up partially fozen mixture and store in smaller containers for later use.)

To serve, remove fruit juice mixture from freezer. Let stand at room temperature for 5 to 10 minutes if mixture contains liquor or about 30 minutes if mixture contains no liquor.

Draw a large spoon across surface of frozen mixture to make slush. Spoon slush into each glass. Slowly pour in carbonated water, using equal amounts of slush and carbonated water.

Or, spoon slush mixture into a punch bowl. Add carbonated water, pouring down side of bowl. Stir gently. Makes about 14 cups punch with liquor or 12½ cups punch without liquor.

Frosty Morn Mocha

Pictured on page 111.

6 squares (6 ounces) unsweetened chocolate, chopped
9 cups milk
6 cups strong coffee
2 cups sugar
1 tablespoon ground cinnamon

In a heavy 6-quart Dutch oven melt chocolate over low heat, stirring constantly. Add milk, coffee, sugar, and cinnamon. Cook and stir till mixture is heated through. Just before serving, whip to a froth. Pour into a 6-quart crockery cooker. Keep warm on the low-heat setting. Serves 20.

Winter's Day Fruit Soup

Pictured on page 108.

6 cups water
1 8-ounce package mixed dried fruit
1 6-ounce can frozen unsweetened apple juice concentrate, thawed
½ cup halved dried figs
½ cup sugar
3 tablespoons quick-cooking tapioca
3 to 4 inches stick cinnamon
3 whole allspice
1 cup frozen unsweetened pitted sour red cherries

Cut up any large pieces of dried fruit. In a Dutch oven or large kettle stir together the water, mixed fruit, apple juice concentrate, figs, sugar, tapioca, stick cinnamon, and allspice.

Bring to boiling. Reduce heat and simmer, covered, for 8 to 10 minutes. Add cherries and heat through. Remove spices. Serve warm. Makes 12 servings.

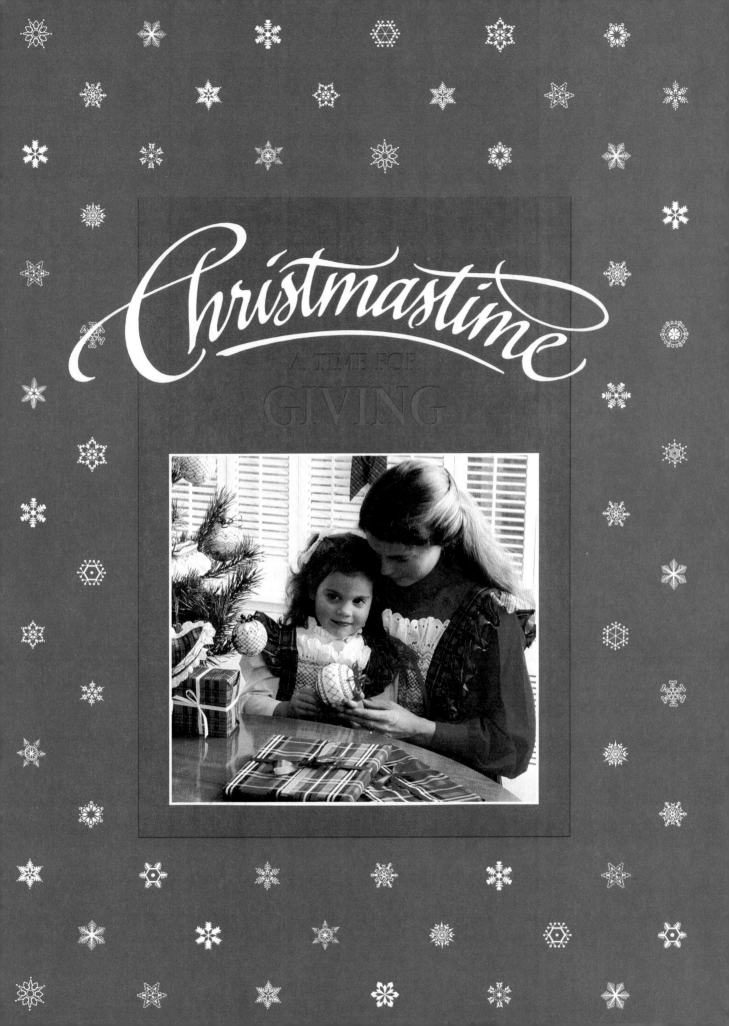

Christmastime

A TIME FOR
GIVING

The Joy of Giving

Somehow not only for Christmas
 But all the long year through,
The joy that you give to others
 Is the joy that comes back to you.
And the more you spend in blessing
 The poor and lonely and sad,
The more of your heart's possessing
 Returns to make you glad.

—*John Greenleaf Whittier*

Trouble at the Inn
—Dina Donohue

For years now whenever Christmas pageants are talked about in a certain little town in the Mid-west, someone is sure to mention the name of Wallace Purling. Wally's performance in one annual production of the Nativity play has slipped into the realm of legend. But the old-timers who were in the audience that night never tire of recalling exactly what happened.

Wally was nine that year and in the second grade, though he should have been in the fourth. Most people in town knew that he had difficulty in keeping up. He was big and clumsy, slow in movement and mind. Still, Wally was well liked by the other children in his class, all of whom were smaller than he, though the boys had trouble hiding their irritation when Wally would ask to play ball with them or any game, for that matter, in which winning was important.

Most often they'd find a way to keep him out but Wally would hang around anyway—not sulking, just hoping. He was always a helpful boy, a willing and smiling one, and the natural protector, paradoxically, of the underdog. Sometimes if the older boys chased the younger ones away, it would always be Wally who'd say, "Can't they stay? They're no bother."

Wally fancied the idea of being a shepherd with a flute in the Christmas pageant that year, but the play's director, Miss Lumbard, assigned him to a more important role. After all, she reasoned, the Innkeeper did not have too many lines, and Wally's size would make his refusal of lodging to Joseph more forceful.

And so it happened that the usual large, partisan audience gathered for the town's yearly extravaganza of crooks and crèches, of beards, crowns, halos and a whole stageful of squeaky voices. No one on stage or off was more caught up in the magic of the night than Wallace Purling. They said later that he stood in the wings and watched the performance with such fascination that from time to time Miss Lumbard had to make sure he didn't wander onstage before his cue.

Then the time came when Joseph appeared, slowly, tenderly guiding Mary to the door of the inn. Joseph knocked hard on the wooden door set into the painted backdrop. Wally the Innkeeper was there, waiting.

"What do you want?" Wally said, swinging the door open with a brusque gesture.

"We seek lodging."

"Seek it elsewhere." Wally looked straight ahead but spoke vigorously. "The inn is filled."

"Sir, we have asked everywhere in vain. We have traveled far and are very weary."

"There is no room in this inn for you." Wally looked properly stern.

"Please, good innkeeper, this is my wife, Mary. She is heavy with child and needs a place to rest. Surely you must have some small corner for her. She is so tired."

Now, for the first time, the Innkeeper relaxed his stiff stance and looked down at Mary. With that, there was a long pause, long enough to make the audience a bit tense with embarrassment.

"No! Begone!" the prompter whispered from the wings.

"No!" Wally repeated automatically. "Begone!"

Joseph sadly placed his arm around Mary and Mary laid her head upon her husband's shoulder and the two of them started to move away. The Innkeeper did not return inside his inn, however. Wally stood there in the doorway, watching the forlorn couple. His mouth was open, his brow creased with concern, his eyes filling unmistakably with tears.

And suddenly this Christmas pageant became different from all others.

"Don't go, Joseph," Wally called out. "Bring Mary back." And Wallace Purling's face grew into a bright smile. "You can have *my* room."

Some people in town thought that the pageant had been ruined. Yet there were others—many, many others—who considered it the most Christmas of all Christmas pageants they had ever seen.

That Ageless Magic

—by Loren Young

One recent Christmas I was visiting my parents who live in a mining community in West Virginia. Times were bad; many of the mines had been shut down. As I walked down to the main part of the town to pick up a few last minute things, I noticed a lame man seated on the cold sidewalk. He had a small tin cup which he held up, hopefully, but few people noticed him—or if they did, they didn't let on.

I could see that one leg was missing. Not an unusual sight in a mining community, but a heartbreaking sight—especially on Christmas Eve.

I started toward him reaching into my pocket. In front of me, a young couple stopped near the lame man. The husband, obviously a miner, and his wife were talking in half whispers.

"Please, please," she was saying. He grimaced, unsure.

"We have our Christmas for us and the kids in these bags," she pleaded. "Let's do it, please." The young husband looked down at his wife. Slowly, a smile came over his face and he agreed.

"But we'll have to walk home 'cause I just saved enough for bus fare."

Reaching into her husband's pocket, she pulled out an old black change purse. Then she walked slowly to the lame man and turned the purse upside down. Coins rattled noisily into the old man's cup. "I'm wishin' you a Merry Christmas," she whispered.

Gratefully, the lame man reached out to shake her hand, then her husband's. There was an exchange of small talk before the couple left.

I watched them walk down the street. As they passed the bus station, the husband made a playful start in that direction. Laughing, his wife pulled him back. They were broke and would have to walk home. But I could tell by the bounce in their steps that it would not be a long walk. When they lightened their purse, they also lightened their hearts, and the joy that comes from giving had worked its ageless magic once again.

Storybook Sweatshirts

Spruce up warm winter sweatshirts with delightful appliquéd scenes.

1 Square = 1 Inch

MATERIALS
Christmas cottage sweatshirt
Purchased pink sweatshirt with front pocket
Solid and print fabric scraps in light blue, turquoise, pink, lavender, magenta, purple, and medium green
Scrap of green rickrack
Nonwoven lightweight fusible interfacing
One small pink bow button
One small pink round button
Tissue paper; marking pen
Snowman sweatshirt
Purchased lavender sweatshirt
Fabric scraps in light blue, green, silver metallic, pink, and magenta
Nonwoven lightweight fusible interfacing
Black embroidery floss
One small pink pom-pom
Two small green buttons
Water-erasable marking pen

INSTRUCTIONS
Enlarge the patterns, *right,* onto paper. Cut out the individual pieces for patterns.

Note: For the cottage, cut whole cottage levels; small pieces will be appliquéd on top. For the snowman sweatshirt, cut the entire trees from green fabric and the entire snowman from light blue fabric. Other pieces will be stitched over these base pieces.

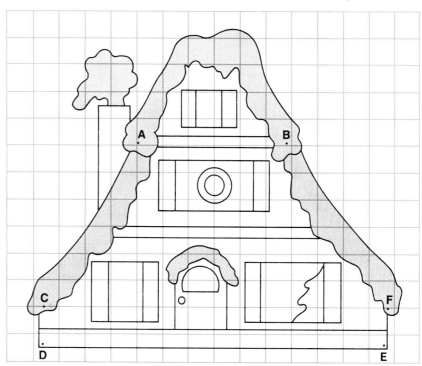

Cut all shaded areas (see patterns) from light blue fabric. Cut remaining pieces from colored scraps, referring to the photograph for color selection.

SNOWMAN: Baste the pieces in place on the sweatshirt front; appliqué with closely spaced machine-zigzag stitches, using matching thread.

COTTAGE: Appliqué the chimney to the sweatshirt, aligning it with the edge of the pocket.

Remove the pocket and appliqué the cottage to it, using closely spaced machine-zigzag stitches and matching thread.

When the appliqué is complete, zigzag-stitch the pocket to the sweatshirt from A to B, C to D, and E to F. Restitch over the outer edges of the snow at the bottom sides of the pocket.

To make the cottage wreath, braid pieces of rickrack into a circle; join the ends. Hand-stitch in place. Add a button bow; sew button to door.

Simply Spectacular Gifts

Even if you're short on time and money, you can create a Santa's sackful of gifts to delight all the children on your Christmas list.

Star-Appliquéd Slippers

Slippers are for children's sizes 2, 4, and 6.

MATERIALS
⅜ yard of red prequilted fabric
⅜ yard of white fur fabric
1⅔ yards of ⅜-inch-wide red grosgrain ribbon
Silver fabric scrap
Fusible interfacing scrap

INSTRUCTIONS
Note: The pattern, *opposite,* includes small, medium, and large sizes, and ¼-inch seam allowances. Sew seams with right sides facing, unless otherwise indicated.

Enlarge patterns onto paper. Cut slipper pieces from quilted fabric, flopping pattern for second slipper. Cut stars from interfacing and silver scraps. Fuse and satin-stitch stars to quilted fabric.

With wrong sides facing, machine-baste fur to sole around outer edges. Sew fur to the slipper back around top and sides; turn to right side; machine-baste the bottom edges together.

Matching centers, sew back to sole. Then sew front to sole around toe area (front overlaps back about 1½ inches). Turn slipper right side out.

Cut ribbon in half; center ribbon at slipper back and stitch down. Fold down cuff; tack edges of cuff to slipper front and thread ribbon under cuffs to front; tie ribbon into bow. Repeat process for the other slipper.

Snow Babies

Finished size is 8 inches tall.

MATERIALS *(for one snow baby)*
Two 9-inch squares of fleece
Small amount of polyester fiberfill
Glitter spray; white glitter
1½-inch-diameter wooden bead
Hat pom-pom
Acrylic paints; glue

INSTRUCTIONS
Enlarge the patterns, *opposite,* onto paper; cut out. On one fleece square, draw around the pattern with pencil. Pin to remaining fleece square and machine-sew around perimeter, leaving an opening for turning. Turn baby right side out; stuff softly.

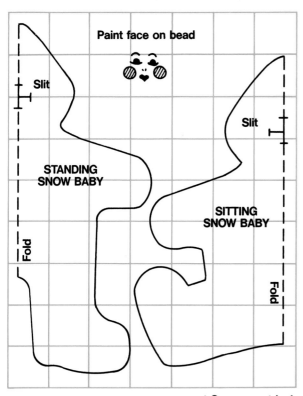

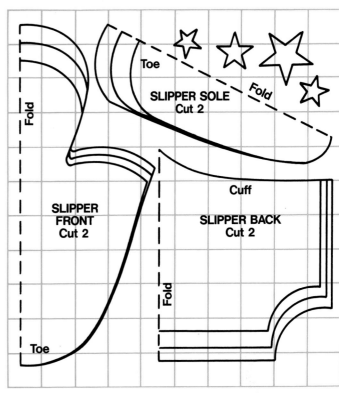

For face, cut slits (see pattern) in fleece; glue bead inside head. When dry, paint face with acrylics.

To finish, glue pom-pom on hat top and a circle of fiberfill around face for fur. Spray snow baby with glitter spray and sprinkle with white glitter.

See-Through Stocking

Finished size is 14 inches tall.

MATERIALS

Two 11x15-inch rectangles of clear tablecloth plastic (available at fabric stores)
3 yards of silver cording
White thread
12-inch square of white adhesive-backed plastic
Metal stars (available at costume supply stores)
Silver beads
1 yard of 3-inch-wide white florist's ribbon

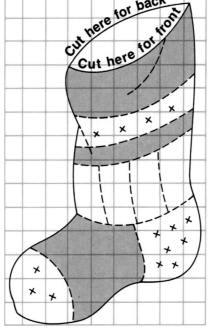

INSTRUCTIONS

Enlarge the pattern, *above,* onto tissue paper. Copy it again, making two tissue-paper patterns.

Tape one tissue behind a plastic rectangle (stocking front). Hand-sew metal stars and beads on Xs (or use star stickers). Tear the tissue away gently, keeping it all in one piece.

Trace the shaded shapes of the pattern onto the wrong side of the white plastic, following the tissue-paper pattern.

Cut out the white plastic pieces and adhere them to the inside of the stocking front.

Zigzag-stitch silver cord over all interior lines to decorate the stocking front. Repeat the process to outline the top edge of the stocking.

Lay the stocking front over the *remaining* plastic rectangle. Tape both layers of plastic to the second tissue pattern.

Zigzag-stitch cording around the entire stocking edge, beginning at the bow corner and leaving a 3-inch end for a hanger. Leave another 3-inch end after finishing the stitch line. Tie the ends into a hanger.

Remove the tissue and cut out the stocking ¼ inch beyond the outer stitch line. Add a large florist's-ribbon bow.

Star-Studded Sleepwear

Big Dipper pillowcases and star-stamped nightshirts will dazzle the reluctant nap takers on your Christmas list.

Big Dipper Pillowcases

MATERIALS
White cotton pillowcases
Charcoal stick; wax
Double boiler; paper cups
Stiff-bristle paintbrush
Scrap of cardboard; newspaper
One package of Royal Blue
    RIT Dye

INSTRUCTIONS
Open seams on pillowcases; wash. With charcoal, outline stars in the Big Dipper formation (see an encyclopedia for Big Dipper constellation). Melt wax in double boiler · (keep temperature just above melting).

Place fabric on cardboard. Using brush, fill in stars with wax. Lift fabric off cardboard every few brushstrokes to prevent sticking. After waxing one side, reverse the fabric and rewax the design.

When wax is hard, prepare dye according to package directions. Wet fabric and, with as little crumpling as possible, immerse in dyebath. Dye until fabric is slightly darker than desired shade.

Rinse fabric in hot water, then cooler water, until the water runs clear; hang to dry.

To remove wax, place fabric between several sheets of newspaper or paper towels, and press with medium-hot iron. As paper absorbs wax, replace with fresh paper and continue ironing.

Finish by sewing seams back into pillowcases.

Star Nightshirts

MATERIALS
Purchased nightshirts
White fabric paint; brush
Metallic stars or paper star
    pattern

INSTRUCTIONS
Draw around the metallic star or pattern, creating an overall design on the nightshirts. Fill in the stars with fabric paint, following paint manufacturer's instructions; let dry. Heat-set paint with iron.

Santa's Kitchen Workshop

Cinnamon cutouts are fun to make, and they add
a holiday scent to any room where they are used.
Make plenty to hang on the Christmas tree, on door
wreaths, and in kitchen windows. Or create a cinnamon
mobile following the suggestions on these pages.

Cinnamon Ornaments

MATERIALS
1 cup of ground cinnamon
4 tablespoons of white glue
¾ to 1 cup of water
Rolling pin
Cookie cutters
Cookie sheet
Toothpick
Waxed paper
Acrylic paint
Artist's brush

1

2

INSTRUCTIONS

Stir together 1 cup of cinnamon, 4 tablespoons of glue, and ¾ cup of water. The dough should be as thick as cookie dough.

Keep the dough in the refrigerator for 2 hours. Then, sprinkle cinnamon on your work surface. Spoon the chilled dough from the bowl onto the cinnamon. Use your fingers and hands to knead the dough until it is smooth. Ask an adult to show you how to knead dough if you have not done it before.

3

Sprinkle more cinnamon on the work surface. Roll the dough to about a ¼-inch thickness. Cut out the shapes with cookie cutters.

You can use cookie cutters in any shapes and sizes. You may want to use a theme for your ornaments, such as barnyard animals. Or use cutters that remind you of Christmas, such as stars, trees, and bells. You could cut all your ornaments from one shape, too, making each one unique in the way you decorate it.

4

To dry the shapes, lay them on waxed paper at room temperature and turn them over twice a day for four days. To speed up the drying, bake the ornaments on a cookie sheet in a warm oven for 2 hours.

5

Before you dry the shapes, poke a hole in the top of each shape, using a plastic straw. The circle of dough will pull out when the straw is removed. When the shapes are dry, thread ribbon through the holes for hangers.

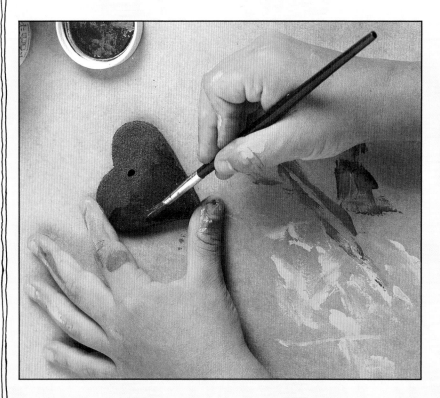

To decorate the ornaments, refer to the photograph on this page, or create your own designs, using storybooks or wrapping paper for ideas. Use acrylic paints and an artist's brush to decorate the shapes. Let each color dry before you add the next color.

Cinnamon Mobile

MATERIALS
Five cinnamon ornaments
Wire or plastic clothes hanger
Yarn; ribbon

INSTRUCTIONS
Another great project you can make from cinnamon shapes is this quick-as-a-wink mobile.

Wrap a wire or plastic clothes hanger with yarn or ribbon. Tie it with a bow at the top. Thread narrow ribbons in matching or contrasting colors through the holes in the tops of the ornaments. Hang five of the different shapes along the bottom of the hanger.

Leave the cinnamon cutouts unpainted or decorate them like the ones pictured here.

7

As the ornaments dry, they will shrink slightly, and the edges may curl. You can't prevent the shrinkage, but you can keep the ornaments from curling by frequently turning them over during the drying process.

Purchased-Package Fix-Ups

With a little imagination, you can create simply
sensational packages from purchased bags and boxes.

Holiday Packages

MATERIALS

Glazed paper gift bags with or
without handles
Glazed cardboard gift boxes
Scraps of ribbon
Metallic paper adhesive letters
Trims for boxes (jingle bells,
stickers, candles)
Florist's wire; glue
Metallic glitter; ornament

INSTRUCTIONS

GREETING BOX: Affix letters on box top to create greeting. Add sticker trims. Glue on ribbon bows or attach jingle bells with florist's wire.

CANDLE-TRIMMED BOX: Twist together the wicks of two pairs of hand-dipped candles. Wire the wicks together, then wire them to the top of the box. Add a bow to conceal the wire.

GLITTER STAR BAG: Lay out bag on a newspaper or in a shallow box. Drizzle glue onto bag front, making a star design. Shake glitter onto glue until all the glue is covered thoroughly. Let glue set; shake off excess glitter onto newspaper or into box. Return glitter to jar.

ORNAMENT BAG: Attach ribbon to an ornament; tape it to the outside of the bag.

BELL-AND-BOW BAG: Tie a big plaid bow onto bell with clapper. Wire bow and bell to front of glazed paper bag.

Kids' Gift Packages

MATERIALS

Glazed paper bags in assorted colors, with or without handles
Stick candy
Pencils with novelty trims
White glue; tissue paper
Glitter in assorted colors

INSTRUCTIONS

GLITTER BAG: Lay out bag on newspaper or in a shallow box. Drizzle glue onto bag front in an abstract design. Shake glitter onto glue until all glue is covered thoroughly. Let glue set; shake off excess glitter onto newspaper or into box. Return glitter to container.

CANDY AND PENCIL BAG: Fold over the top edge of a bag to form a 2½- to 3-inch flap. Using a sharp knife or crafts knife, make two vertical slits through both the flap and bag; each slit should be about 1½ inches long. (See the photograph, *below,* for reference.)

Slide a stick of candy, a pencil, or a pen through the slits to keep the bag closed.

FILLING THE BAGS: To protect your gift and add color, too, fill the bag with colored tissue paper, shredded excelsior, or confetti. You might want to try using the color comics section of your local newspaper. For a final touch, decorate or seal your bags with shiny stickers, available at variety stores.

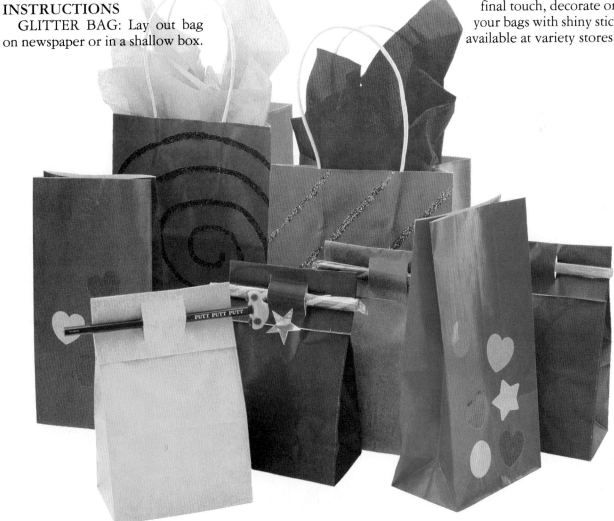

The Erector Set

—Richard H. Schneider

Like many small brothers we were sworn enemies. I'd ride *his* bike, he'd touch *my* train and war was declared. Christmas was a temporary truce for Herb and me.

Our family celebrated it in Old World fashion—on Christmas Eve. Returning from church services, our parents would usher us through the darkened parlor past the tree, unseen but pungently there, to the kitchen where we'd excitedly wait while dad went out to help Kriss Kringle find our house. The doorbell's ring would signal our burst into the parlor. And there Santa would be in full costume—the tree now aglow and the furniture sagging with uncles, aunts and grandparents.

After Santa heard our lies about being "good boys," we'd plunge into our gifts. For Christmas was for *us*—its joy measured by what we *got*.

I was seven the Christmas I'll never forget.

Amid my spoils I came across a clumsily wrapped little package. Unopened in my hand, it already had a strange quality about it. Instinctively I knew it wasn't from my parents.

I turned to my brother; he was watching me.

"It's from me," he said in awe.

Stunned, I slowly opened it.

It was a 25-cent erector set.

Herb had spent all Saturday afternoon picking it out. It represented a half day's work delivering groceries.

His face was aglow with a strange new light of eagerness and concern.

I've long forgotten the other things I got that Christmas Eve. But I'll never forget that little erector set.

For along with it, I'd been given a first vision of God's great gift—that divine joy which floods the heart of the *giver*.

Long Walk Part of Gift

—by Gerald Horton Bath

The African boy listened carefully as the teacher explained why it is that Christians give presents to each other on Christmas day. "The gift is an expression of our joy over the birth of Jesus and our friendship for each other," she said.

When Christmas day came, the boy brought the teacher a sea shell of lustrous beauty. "Where did you ever find such a beautiful shell?" the teacher asked as she gently fingered the gift.

The youth told her that there was only one spot where such extraordinary shells could be found. When he named the place, a certain bay several miles away, the teacher was left speechless.

"Why . . . why, it's gorgeous . . . wonderful, but you shouldn't have gone all that way to get a gift for me."

His eyes brightening, the boy answered, "Long walk part of gift."

Basketfuls of Gifts
From the Kitchen

Charm any food aficionados on your Christmas list with
treats you make yourself. Family and friends will
appreciate the sophisticated flavors as well as the
thought that accompanies each gift. It's a delicious way
to wish someone special a "Merry Christmas . . . from
Our House to Your House."

Seafood Sandwich Ring

Pictured on pages 140–141.

 1 cup all-purpose flour
 1 package active dry yeast
 ¾ cup milk
 2 tablespoons brown sugar
 1 tablespoon shortening
 1 to 1½ cups whole wheat
      flour
 1 7-ounce can crabmeat,
      drained, flaked, and
      cartilage removed
 1 4½-ounce can shrimp,
      rinsed, drained, and
      cut up
 ½ cup snipped watercress
 ⅓ cup mayonnaise *or* salad
      dressing
 3 tablespoons margarine *or*
      butter, softened
 2 tablespoons lemon juice
 2 ounces cream cheese
      Milk

Mix all-purpose flour and yeast. Heat and stir milk, brown sugar, shortening, and ½ teaspoon *salt* just till warm (115° to 120°) and shortening almosts melts. Add to yeast mixture. Beat with electric mixer on low speed for ½ minute, scraping bowl. Beat 3 minutes on high speed. Stir in as much whole wheat flour as you can.

Turn out onto a floured surface. Knead in enough remaining whole wheat flour to make a moderately stiff dough that is smooth and elastic (6 to 8 minutes). Place in a greased bowl; turn once. Cover; let rise till double (1 to 1¼ hours). Punch down. Turn out onto a floured surface. Cover; let rest 10 minutes.

Shape into a 20-inch-long rope. Place in a greased 5-cup oven-proof ring mold. Cover; let rise till double (about 30 minutes). Bake in a 375° oven for 20 to 25 minutes, covering with foil the last 5 minutes. Remove from pan. Cool.

For filling, combine crabmeat, shrimp, watercress, mayonnaise, margarine, and lemon juice. If necessary, level the flat side of bread ring using a long sharp knife. Cut a ¼-inch-thick slice from flat side and set aside. Hollow out remaining bread ring with a spoon, leaving a ¼-inch-thick shell. Spoon filling into bread shell. Replace flat side of bread.

Invert sandwich ring onto a plate. Beat cream cheese with a little milk (about 4 teaspoons) to a drizzling consistency. Drizzle atop ring. Chill 2 hours or till cheese mixture is set. Wrap in clear plastic wrap. Makes 1 ring.

Gift Instructions: Store, covered, in the refrigerator for up to 2 days.

Almond Butter Beverage Mix

Pictured on pages 140–141.

 4 cups packed brown sugar
 1 cup butter, softened
 ⅔ cup Amaretto
 ½ cup powdered nondairy
      creamer
 1 teaspoon ground cinnamon
 1 teaspoon ground allspice

Beat together all ingredients till well combined. Place in a covered container. Chill. Makes 5 cups.

Gift Instructions: Store in refrigerator up to 1 month. For each serving, spoon *1 tablespoon* chilled mix into a mug. Add 6 ounces hot *coffee, cocoa, or milk.* Serve at once.

Marinated Vegetables

Pictured on pages 140–141.

 ⅔ cup lemon juice
 ⅓ cup salad oil
 ⅓ cup olive oil
 1 tablespoon snipped chives
 1 tablespoon grated
      gingerroot
 1 tablespoon light corn syrup
 1 9-ounce package frozen
      artichoke hearts, thawed
 1 cup frozen crinkle-cut
      carrots, thawed
 1 cup cherry tomatoes,
      halved
 1 10-ounce package frozen
      peas, thawed
 1 cup frozen small whole
      onions, thawed

For marinade, in a screw-top jar combine lemon juice, salad oil, olive oil, chives, gingerroot, corn syrup, and ¾ teaspoon *salt.* Cover; shake well. Set marinade aside.

In three 1-pint containers with tight-fitting lids, layer vegetables in this order: artichokes, carrots, tomato halves (cut side out), peas, and onions. Add enough marinade to cover vegetables. Cover; refrigerate. Makes 3 pints.

Gift Instructions: Store, covered, in refrigerator up to 3 days.

Black Forest Christmas Cakes

Pictured on pages 140–141.

1 cup red candied cherries, halved
1½ cups coarsely chopped pecans
1 package 1-layer-size chocolate cake mix
3 eggs
⅓ cup cherry brandy
2 tablespoons cooking oil
1 teaspoon vanilla
¼ cup cherry brandy
3 tablespoons sugar
Cherry Hard Sauce

Grease and flour six 1-cup fluted tube pans or twenty-four ¼-cup ovenproof molds. Place a cherry half, rounded side down, in the bottom of each. Set aside. Chop the remaining cherries; toss with pecans and *2 tablespoons* dry cake mix. Set aside.

Beat eggs with an electric mixer on high speed for 4 to 5 minutes or till thick and lemon colored. Gradually add the ⅓ cup brandy, oil, and vanilla. Beat well. Add dry cake mix; beat on low speed for 1 minute. Stir cherry-nut mixture into cake batter.

Transfer batter to prepared pans, filling about half full. Bake in a 350° oven for 25 to 30 minutes or till done. Place pans on wire racks. Cool 10 minutes. Remove from pans; cool completely.

Meanwhile, heat together the ¼ cup brandy and sugar till sugar dissolves. Using a fork, pierce the cakes. Slowly spoon the brandy-sugar mixture over baked cakes. Wrap each cake in clear plastic wrap; refrigerate. For gift-giving, include Cherry Hard Sauce with each cake. Makes 6.

Cherry Hard Sauce: Beat together 1 cup sifted *powdered sugar* and ¼ cup softened *margarine or butter.* Beat in ½ teaspoon *cherry brandy or vanilla.* Dollop hard sauce into small candy cups.

Gift Instructions: Store cakes and hard sauce, covered, in refrigerator for up to 1 week.

Three-Fruit Chutney

Pictured on pages 140–141.

2 cups cranberries
1 cup packed brown sugar
1 cup chopped apple
⅓ cup vinegar
¼ cup water
¼ cup snipped dried apricots
¼ teaspoon salt
⅛ teaspoon ground ginger
⅛ teaspoon ground allspice
⅛ teaspoon dry mustard

Combine all ingredients. Bring to boiling. Reduce heat and simmer, uncovered, for 15 minutes, stirring frequently. Spoon into refrigerator or freezer containers. Cover, seal, label, and refrigerate or freeze. Makes 2 cups.

Gift Instructions: Store, covered, in refrigerator for up to 3 months or in freezer for up to 6 months.

Hickory-Smoked Duck

Pictured on pages 140–141.

8 cups hickory chips (about 1 pound)
1 4- to 5-pound whole domestic duckling *or* one 5- to 6-pound turkey breast
2 cups water

About 1 hour before cooking, soak hickory chips in enough water to cover. Rinse duck or turkey breast. Pat dry. Skewer neck skin to back. Tie legs securely to tail. Twist wing tips under. For duck, prick skin well all over.

In a covered grill arrange slow coals around a foil drip pan in firebox. Add the 2 cups water to drip pan. Drain hickory chips; sprinkle about *half* of the chips over the coals. Place duck, breast side up, or turkey, skin side up, on grill rack over drip pan.

Lower grill hood. Smoke the duck for 2 to 2¼ hours or smoke the turkey breast for 3 to 3½ hours or till internal temperature of duck or turkey reaches 180°. Occasionally brush turkey breast with cooking oil (not necessary for duck). Add dampened hickory chips every 30 minutes. Cool. Store smoked bird, covered, in refrigerator. Make 4 to 6 servings.

Gift Instructions: Store, covered, in refrigerator for up to 1 week.

A Basketful of Giving

The beauty of baskets for holiday giving lies in their versatility. Not only does the basket itself become an appreciated gift, but all that it holds adds to the merriment, too.

Baskets come in such a wide range of shapes, sizes, and materials that you can find one suited to whatever gift you care to give. Look for baskets in out-of-the-way places, such as antique stores, crafts shops, and establishments that sell miniatures or specialty gift items. The unexpected places will yield the most delightful results.

Keep your eyes open for other surprising containers, too, such as Chinese takeout-style boxes for tiny treasures, or colorful pails that could be put to use in a child's room after Christmas is over.

If you can't find just the basket you want, you might create your own. With the help of instructions or classes from your local crafts store, you can make several country-style reed baskets in a single weekend.

The gifts that are suitable for giving in baskets are just as unlimited as the containers themselves. Food, of course, is an excellent choice for basket giving. Wrapped and beribboned, jars of homemade preserves, cookies, or candies are a special treat. But don't let your imagination stop there. Consider theme gifts that tie the basket and the gifts together.

For instance, purchase a summertime picnic hamper to hold a Christmas turkey and wine for a special family gift. Or choose a rustic basket made of grapevines or twigs, then fill it with bundles of dried herbs and flowers, plus flower seeds and gardening tools, for a springtime reminder in the cold winter months.

One of the joys of basket giving is the array of gifts you can give all at once. Look for little soaps, scented sprays, and packets of potpourri, for instance, then arrange them in layers of excelsior and tissue paper for a Christmas morning treasure hunt. Even people who seem to have everything will appreciate smaller items that add up to such a unique gift.

For Christmas decorating, you can turn the baskets themselves into charming tree ornaments or package trims, too. For a nature lover, fill a tiny basket with straw, perch a bird ornament on the edge, then hang the "nest" from the tree with ribbon. Or for a child, fill a miniature basket with candies and trinkets, then tie it to the tree with colorful, namesake shoelaces.

With a basketful of giving, you can personalize your presents to the needs and interests of everyone on your Christmas list. That type of thoughtfulness is what makes basket gift-giving the most special of all.

Tarragon-Wine Mustard Sauce

½ cup Dijon-style mustard
⅓ cup olive oil *or* cooking oil
¼ cup white vinegar
¼ cup dry white wine
2 tablespoons dry mustard
1 teaspoon dried basil, crushed
1 teaspoon dried tarragon, crushed

In a small mixing bowl stir together Dijon-style mustard, oil, vinegar, white wine, dry mustard, basil, and tarragon. Transfer to small attractive jars. Cover; label. Makes 1⅓ cups mustard mixture.
Gift instructions: Serve with chilled meats, as a sauce on vegetables, or use to baste meats while cooking.

Glorious Morning Muffins

2 cups all-purpose flour
1¼ cups sugar
2 teaspoons baking soda
2 teaspoons ground cinnamon
1½ cups finely shredded carrot
1½ cups peeled and shredded apple (1 large apple)
¾ cup coconut
½ cup snipped pitted dates
½ cup chopped pecans
3 beaten eggs
1 cup cooking oil
½ teaspoon vanilla

Combine flour, sugar, soda, cinnamon, and ½ teaspoon *salt.* Combine carrot, apple, coconut, dates, and pecans; stir in beaten eggs, oil, and vanilla. Add to dry ingredients, stirring till moistened.

Grease or line muffin pans with paper bake cups. Spoon batter into prepared muffin pans. Bake in a 375° oven for 18 to 20 minutes. Remove from pans; cool on wire racks. Package for giving as desired. Makes about 24.
Gift Instructions: Serve muffins with whipped cream cheese.

Bouquet Garni Jelly

6½ cups sugar
2 cups water
1 cup red wine vinegar
3 Bouquet Garni
1 6-ounce package liquid fruit pectin (2 foil pouches)

In a saucepan combine sugar, water, vinegar, and Bouquet Garni. Bring to a full rolling boil, stirring to dissolve sugar. Stir in the pectin. Bring to a full rolling boil again. Boil hard for 1 minute. Discard Bouquet Garni.

Pour the hot liquid into clean, hot jelly jars, leaving a ¼-inch headspace. Seal jars, using canning lids, or paraffin and metal lids. Makes 7 half-pints.

Bouquet Garni: Cut a small square from several thicknesses of cheesecloth. Place 4 sprigs *parsley;* 2 cloves *garlic,* halved; 2 teaspoons snipped fresh *thyme or* ¾ teaspoon dried *thyme;* and 1 *bay leaf* in center of the cheesecloth. Bring corners of cheesecloth together. Tie with string. Makes 1.
Gift Instructions: Store, covered, after opening.

Holiday Ginger Chutney

2 cups packed brown sugar
¾ cup vinegar
½ teaspoon salt
¼ teaspoon ground cinnamon
¼ teaspoon ground red
    pepper
1 lime
1 lemon
1 pound fresh Anjou pears,
    peeled, cored, and
    coarsely chopped
    (about 3 cups)
1 cup chopped green pepper
1 cup chopped sweet red
    pepper
1 cup chopped onion
1 tablespoon chopped
    candied ginger
1 cup light raisins

In a saucepan combine brown sugar, vinegar, salt, cinnamon, and red pepper. Bring to boiling. Reduce heat and simmer, uncovered, for 10 minutes. Finely shred the peel from the lime and lemon. Squeeze juice from each.

In a large bowl combine lime and lemon peels and juices, pears, peppers, onion, and ginger. Add raisins, mixing gently. Add fruit

mixture to hot sugar mixture. Bring to boiling. Reduce heat and simmer, uncovered, about 1 hour or till thick. Ladle at once into hot, clean pint jars, leaving a ¼-inch headspace. Wipe jar rims; adjust lids. Process in boiling water bath for 15 minutes (start timing when water boils). Makes 2 pints.
Gift Instructions: Serve as an accompaniment to cooked ham, poultry, or other meat.

Chocolate Truffles

6 squares (6 ounces)
    semisweet chocolate,
    coarsely chopped
¼ cup butter *or* margarine
3 tablespoons whipping
    cream
1 beaten egg yolk
3 tablespoons Homemade
    Amaretto (see recipe,
    page 147)
1½ pounds semisweet *or* milk
    chocolate dipping
    chocolate *or*
    confectioners' coating

For centers, in a heavy medium saucepan combine the 6 squares semisweet chocolate, butter or margarine, and whipping cream. Cook and stir over low heat till chocolate is melted, stirring constantly. Gradually stir about *half* of the hot mixture into the egg yolk.

Return all of the mixture to the saucepan. Cook and stir over medium heat for 2 minutes. Remove from heat. Stir in the Homemade Amaretto.

Transfer the chocolate mixture to a small mixer bowl. Chill about 1 hour or till mixture is completely cool and is smooth, stirring occasionally. Beat the cooled chocolate mixture with an electric mixer on medium speed till slightly fluffy. Chill about 15 minutes more or till mixture holds its shape. Drop from a level teaspoon onto a waxed-paper-lined baking sheet. Chill about 30 minutes more or till firm.

To dip chocolates, temper dipping chocolate or melt confectioners' coating. Dip centers into the melted chocolate or confectioners' coating. Drizzle with additional melted chocolate or top with chocolate-flavored sprinkles, if desired. Makes 48 candies.

Homemade Amaretto

1½ cups sugar
2 cups water
2 cups vodka
2 cups brandy
2 teaspoons almond extract
¼ teaspoon vanilla

In a medium saucepan combine the sugar and water. Bring to boiling. Reduce heat and simmer, uncovered, for 10 minutes, stirring occasionally. Remove from heat and cool completely.

Stir in the vodka, brandy, almond extract, and vanilla. Transfer to tightly covered bottles or jars. Makes 5½ cups.

Dipped Fruit

2 ounces white
   confectioners' coating
2 ounces milk chocolate
2 ounces German sweet
   cooking chocolate
   Glacéed fruit, strawberries,
   and/or maraschino
   cherries

In separate small saucepans melt the white confectioners' coating, the milk chocolate, and the German sweet cooking chocolate. (*Or,* place in separate small microwave-safe bowls and melt in the microwave oven.)

Using a choice of glacéed or fresh fruits, place one piece of fruit on the end of a wooden skewer. Dip a portion of the fruit into each pan of melted chocolate, forming 3 overlapping layers by dipping deeply into 1 pan of choc- olate, dipping less deeply into the next, and dipping just the tip into the last, allowing chocolate to harden slightly between dippings. Place the dipped fruit on a waxed-paper-lined pan. Chill till firm or up to 2 hours.

Gift Instructions: Serve dipped fresh fruit the same day it is dipped. Store dipped dried fruit, covered, in refrigerator for up to 3 days.

Marvelous Marmalade

2 large tart apples
2 large pears
12 ounces dried apricots,
   snipped (2½ cups)
8 ounces dried light figs,
   stemmed and snipped
   (1⅓ cups)
4 ounces pitted dates,
   chopped (⅔ cup)
½ of a medium orange,
   seeded and chopped
½ of a medium lemon, seeded
   and chopped
1 cup honey
1 cup water
1 cup dry sherry
½ cup kirsch *or* brandy
   Candied Lemon Slices
   (optional)
   Star anise (optional)

Peel, core, and finely chop apples and pears (should have a total of 4 cups). In a 6-quart kettle or Dutch oven combine chopped apples, chopped pears, apricots, figs, dates, orange, lemon, honey, water, dry sherry, and kirsch or brandy. Bring the mixture to boiling, stirring constantly. Boil gently, stirring occasionally, for 20 minutes or till thick and spreadable.

If desired, line 6 hot, clean half-pint jars or 3 pint jars with Candied Lemon Slices. Spoon the marmalade into the jars, leaving a ¼-inch headspace for half-pints or a ½-inch headspace for pint jars. If desired, top each with a star anise. Wipe jar rims and adjust lids. Refrigerate till serving time. Makes 6 half-pints or 3 pints.

Candied Lemon Slices: Cut 2 medium *lemons* into ¼-inch-thick slices. In a 10-inch skillet combine 1 sup *sugar* and ½ cup *water.* Bring to boiling over medium heat. Boil for 2 minutes. Add the lemon slices. Bring to boiling and boil for 5 minutes or till translucent. Let slices cool in syrup. Dry on racks. Makes about 10 slices.

Gift Instructions: Store, covered, in the refrigerator for up to 3 months after opening.

Festive and Fancy Breads

For the time of year when you go all out in your baking, we assembled a bread collection that's the best of the best. With yeast breads like Angel Rolls and Almond Bread Crown, we teamed the ultimate holiday ingredients for these most unforgettable breads.

Rich Yeast Dough

From this basic dough come three delicious bread recipes. Ease the time crunch even further by mixing and freezing the dough up to three months ahead.

6½ cups all-purpose flour
2 packages active dry yeast
1½ cups milk
¾ cup margarine *or* butter
½ cup packed brown sugar
½ teaspoon salt
5 eggs

In a large mixer bowl combine *3 cups* of the flour and yeast. In a medium saucepan heat milk, margarine, sugar, and salt just till warm (115° to 120°) and margarine is almost melted, stirring constantly. Add to flour mixture along with eggs. Beat with an electric mixer on low speed for ½ minute. Beat on high speed for 3 minutes. Stir in remaining flour to make a soft dough.

Place dough in a greased bowl. Grease top of dough lightly. Cover and let rise in a warm place till double (1 to 1½ hours). Stir dough down (it will be sticky). Divide into thirds (1 pound each). Place *each* in a plastic bag. Tie, leaving ample space for expansion. Chill 2 to 24 hours.

To freeze dough: After dividing, wrap in moisture- and vaporproof wrap. Seal, label, and freeze up to 3 months. To use, thaw overnight in the refrigerator.

Starburst Bread

Pictured on pages 148–149.

⅓ recipe Rich Yeast Dough (see recipe, left)
1 egg yolk
1 tablespoon milk
1 teaspoon caraway seed
1 teaspoon fennel seed
1 teaspoon aniseed
½ cup margarine *or* butter, softened

Punch down Rich Yeast Dough. Divide into 8 portions. On a lightly floured surface, roll *each* portion into a 9-inch-long rope. Coil 1 rope and place in the center of a lightly greased baking sheet. Moisten end of *one* of the remaining ropes; press into the center of the coil on the baking sheet. Repeat with remaining ropes, arranging them spoke fashion at equal intervals. Coil up the outer end of each rope once (see photo, below). Curve the middle portion of the dough rope slightly. Cover

and let rise in a warm place till double (30 to 45 minutes).

In a small bowl combine egg yolk and milk; brush over dough. Sprinkle with *½ teaspoon* of each seed. Bake in a 375° oven about 20 minutes or till golden, covering completely with foil after 15 minutes to prevent overbrowning. Remove and cool completely on wire rack.

Meanwhile, in a mortar and pestle, crush the remaining seeds. In a small mixing bowl stir together crushed seeds and margarine or butter. Serve with bread. Makes 12 servings.

Festive Pinwheel Rolls

Pictured on pages 148–149.

⅓ recipe Rich Yeast Dough (see recipe, left)
8 teaspoons margarine *or* butter, softened
¼ cup red raspberry, apricot, *or* cherry preserves
Milk
Finely chopped walnuts *or* pecans

Punch down Rich Yeast Dough. Divide dough in half. Cover and chill *half* of the dough. On a floured surface roll remaining dough into a 15x12½-inch rectangle. Cut rolled dough into three 12½x5-inch rectangles. Spread *one* of the rectangles with *2 teaspoons* of margarine. Top with another rectangle. Repeat with another *2 teaspoons* of margarine and a dough rectangle. With a sharp knife, cut in half lengthwise. Cut crosswise into fifths. (You will have ten 2½-inch squares.)

Place squares 1 inch apart on a greased baking sheet. With the sharp knife, cut 1-inch slits from center to each corner. Spoon about ½ *teaspoon* of preserves in each center. Fold every other point to center to form a pinwheel. Pinch points together (see photo, below). Brush center of each roll with a little milk. Sprinkle a few nuts atop; press down in center to seal. Repeat with remaining dough. Cover; let rise in a warm place for 20 minutes. Gently press closed the tips of any rolls that opened during rising.

Bake in a 375° oven about 12 minutes or till golden. Cool. If desired, spoon additional preserves and sprinkle additional nuts in center of rolls. Makes 20 rolls.

Almond Bread Crown

Pictured on pages 148–149.

⅓ **recipe Rich Yeast Dough**
 (see recipe, opposite)
½ **cup almond paste**
¼ **cup packed brown sugar**
1 **egg**
¾ **cup sifted powdered sugar**
 Milk
¼ **cup sliced almonds,**
 coarsely chopped

Punch down Rich Yeast Dough. Reserve *one-fourth* of the dough. On a lightly floured surface, roll remaining dough into an 18x10-inch rectangle.

Crumble almond paste into a small mixer bowl. Add brown sugar and egg. Beat with an electric mixer on medium speed till mixed. Spread the almond paste mixture over the rolled-out dough to within ½ inch of the edges. Roll up dough from one of the long sides. Moisten and pinch the seam to seal. Roll a 6x3-inch piece of

cardboard into a tube 3 inches high and 1½ inches in diameter; wrap with foil. Grease the outside of the foil and stand the tube up in the center of a greased 9x1½-inch round baking pan. Coil dough roll, seam side down, around tube in pan, pinching ends of dough together to seal.

Roll reserved dough into a 24-inch rope. Lay around the top outside edge of dough in the pan; moisten and pinch ends together to seal. With scissors, snip about halfway through dough rope at 1-inch intervals (see photo, left). Cover; let rise in a warm place till nearly double (about 40 minutes).

Bake in a 350° oven for 20 minutes. Remove foil-covered tube. Bake for 15 to 20 minutes more or till bread sounds hollow when tapped. Cover bread with foil during last 10 minutes of baking to prevent overbrowning. Remove bread from pan. Cool completely on a wire rack.

For glaze, in a small mixing bowl combine powdered sugar and enough milk (about 3 teaspoons) to make a glaze of drizzling consistency. Spoon the glaze over the top of the bread. Sprinkle with almonds. Serves 12.

Honey-Poppy-Seed Brioche

Pictured opposite.

  1 package active dry yeast
¼ cup warm water (105° to 115°)
½ cup margarine *or* butter
¼ cup honey
  4 cups all-purpose flour
½ cup milk
  4 eggs
  1 tablespoon poppy seed

Soften yeast in the ¼ cup warm water. In a large mixer bowl beat together margarine, honey, and ½ teaspoon *salt.* Add *1 cup* of the flour and milk to beaten mixture. Stir till well combined. Separate *one* egg. Cover and refrigerate egg white. Beat yolk and remaining 3 eggs into honey mixture. Add softened yeast; beat well.

Stir in remaining flour and poppy seed till smooth. Transfer to a greased bowl. Cover and let rise till double (about 2 hours). Refrigerate dough up to 24 hours.

Stir dough down. Turn dough out onto a lightly floured surface. Divide dough into quarters; set one portion aside. Divide each of the remaining quarters into 6 pieces, making a total of 18.

Form into balls. Place in 18 greased, individual brioche pans. Divide reserved dough into 18 pieces. Shape into balls. With a floured finger, make an indentation in each large ball. Press a small ball into each indentation.

Beat together reserved egg white and 1 tablespoon *water.* Brush over rolls. Cover and let rise till nearly double (30 to 40

minutes). Bake in a 375° oven for 15 minutes, brushing again after 7 minutes. Makes 18.

To use muffin cups: Prepare dough and divide into quarters as directed above. Set one portion aside. Divide each of the remaining quarters into 8 pieces, for a total of 24. Shape into balls. Place each ball in a greased muffin cup. Divide reserved dough into 24 pieces; shape into balls.

Make an indentation in each large ball. Press a small ball into each indentation. Combine the reserved egg white and 1 tablespoon *water.* Brush over the rolls. Cover and let rise till nearly double (30 to 40 minutes). Bake as directed above. Makes 24.

Lemon-Cheese Crown

Pictured opposite.

3½ to 4 cups all-purpose flour
  1 package active dry yeast
  2 teaspoons finely shredded lemon peel
  1 teaspoon ground cardamom
  1 cup milk
⅓ cup sugar
¼ cup margarine *or* butter
  1 cup finely shredded Edam *or* Swiss cheese
  1 egg
  1 egg yolk
  1 beaten egg white
  1 tablespoon sugar
  1 tablespoon sliced almonds, toasted

Mix *1½ cups* of flour, yeast, lemon peel, and cardamom.

Heat and stir milk, the ⅓ cup sugar, margarine, and ½ teaspoon *salt* just till warm (115° to 120°) and margarine starts to melt. Add to flour mixture. Add cheese, egg, and egg yolk. Beat with electric mixer on low speed for ½ minute, scraping bowl. Beat 3 minutes on high speed. Stir in as much remaining flour as you can.

Turn out onto a floured surface. Knead in enough remaining flour to make a moderately stiff dough that is smooth and elastic (6 to 8 minutes total). Place into greased bowl; turn once. Cover; let rise till double (about 1¼ hours).

Punch dough down. Divide dough into 2 portions, one-third of the dough in one and two-thirds in the other. Cover dough and let rest for 10 minutes.

On a lightly floured surface divide larger portion into 3 pieces. Roll each piece into a 20-inch-long rope. Braid the 3 ropes loosely, starting in center and working out to ends. Place on a greased baking sheet to form a circle. Seal ends together.

Repeat with small piece of dough to form three 18-inch-long ropes, braiding as directed above. Place second braid on top of larger braid. Seal ends together.

Cover; let rise till nearly double (50 to 60 minutes). Brush with egg white. Sprinkle with the 1 tablespoon sugar and almonds.

Bake in a 350° oven for 35 to 40 minutes or till done. Cover with foil after 15 minutes to prevent overbrowning. Makes 1 loaf.

Herb-Cheese Ring

Pictured opposite.

2 to 2½ cups all-purpose
    flour
1 package active dry yeast
¼ cup grated Parmesan
    cheese
1½ cups milk
2 tablespoons honey
2 tablespoons margarine *or*
    butter
¾ teaspoon dried oregano,
    crushed
2 cups whole wheat flour
1 egg
    Sesame seed
    Poppy seed

Mix *1½ cups* all-purpose flour, yeast, and cheese. Heat milk, honey, margarine, oregano, and ½ teaspoon *salt* till warm (115° to 120°) and till margarine almost melts. Add to flour mixture. Beat on low speed for 30 seconds. Beat on high speed for 3 minutes. Stir in whole wheat flour and as much remaining all-purpose flour as possible.

On a lightly floured surface knead in enough remaining all-purpose flour to make a moderately stiff dough that is smooth (6 to 8 minutes total). Place in greased bowl; turn once. Cover; let rise till double (about 1 to 1¼ hours). Punch down; divide in half. Cover; let rest for 10 minutes.

Roll each piece of dough into a 20-inch-long rope. With ropes offset about 3 inches, twist together (see photo, right). Lap ends; seal. Place on greased baking sheet in a circle. Seal ends. Cover; let rise till nearly double (30 to 40 minutes).

Beat egg and 1 tablespoon *water;* brush ring. Sprinkle twists with sesame and poppy seed.

Bake in a 375° oven about 30 minutes or till bread tests done, covering with foil after 15 minutes, if necessary. Cool. Makes 1.

Angel Rolls

Pictured opposite.

3 to 3½ cups all-purpose
    flour
1 package active dry yeast
½ cup milk
¼ cup margarine *or* butter
3 tablespoons sugar
2 eggs
1 tablespoon finely shredded
    orange peel
¼ cup orange juice
½ cup sifted powdered sugar
    Milk

Mix *1 cup* flour and yeast. Heat milk, margarine, sugar, and ¼ teaspoon *salt* just till warm (115° to 120°) and till margarine almost melts. Add to flour mixture along with eggs, peel, and juice. Beat on low speed for 30 seconds. Beat on high speed for 3 minutes. Stir in as much remaining flour as you can. Knead in enough remaining flour to make a moderately soft dough that is smooth (3 to 5 minutes total). Place into greased bowl; turn once. Cover; let rise till double (about 1 hour). Punch down. Cover; let rest 10 minutes.

On a floured surface, roll dough into 15x12-inch rectangle. Cut lengthwise into three 4-inch strips, then crosswise into 3-inch strips to make 15 rectangles. On each rectangle make a diagonal

cut from each corner to within ½ inch of center. Place 2 inches apart on greased baking sheets. To shape angels, remove one short triangle from rectangle of dough. Form into a ball for head. Flatten slightly; set aside. For wings, pull long side of triangles upward and outward slightly, indenting sides. Put head in place (see photo, above). Cover; let rise till nearly double (about 30 minutes).

Bake in a 375° oven for 8 to 10 minutes or till done. Combine powdered sugar and about *2 teaspoons* milk. Using a cake decorating tube, decorate cooled angels as desired. Makes 15.

Ribbon Coffee Cake

Pictured opposite.

3¼ to 3¾ cups all-purpose
    flour
1 package active dry yeast
1 3-ounce package cream
    cheese, cut up
¾ cup milk
½ cup sugar
3 tablespoons margarine *or*
    butter
½ teaspoon salt
1 egg
½ cup chopped walnuts
½ cup chopped red candied
    cherries
¼ cup sugar
    Powdered Sugar Icing

In a large mixer bowl stir together *1½ cups* of the flour and the yeast. In a saucepan heat cream cheese, milk, the ½ cup sugar, margarine, and salt just till warm (115° to 120°) and cream cheese is almost melted, stirring constantly. Add to dry ingredients along with egg. Beat with an electric mixer on low speed for 30 seconds, scraping sides of bowl constantly. Beat on high speed for 3 minutes. Using a spoon, stir in as much of the remaining flour as you can to make a soft dough.

Turn out onto a lightly floured surface. Knead in enough of the remaining flour to make a moderately soft dough that is smooth and elastic (3 to 5 minutes total). Shape into a ball. Place in a lightly greased bowl, turning once to grease surface. Cover and let rise

in a warm place till double (about 1 to 1½ hours).

Punch dough down. Shape into a ball. Cover and let rest for 10 minutes. On a lightly floured surface roll into a 16x10-inch rectangle. Brush dough with *water.* Combine nuts, cherries, and the ¼ cup sugar; sprinkle over dough. Roll up, jelly-roll style, starting with long side. Pinch to seal. Place roll, seam side down, on a greased baking sheet.

To form bow, starting at 1 end, use a sharp knife to make an 8-inch lengthwise cut completely through roll. Turn cut sides up and coil each half outward, tucking ends under at center to form the loops of the bow. From other end, make a 6-inch cut completely through (a 2-inch portion in center will be left uncut). Turn cut

sides up and spread the 2 pieces apart slightly to form ends of the bow (see photo, above).

Cover and let rise till nearly double (30 to 45 minutes). Bake in a 325° oven for 30 to 35 minutes or till no longer doughy in thickest part. If necessary, cover with foil to prevent overbrowning. Remove from baking sheet. Cool on wire rack.

Spread Powdered Sugar Icing over center portion of bread. If desired, allow icing to dry. Pipe a bow on top. Drizzle remaining icing over bread. Makes 1.

Powdered Sugar Icing: Stir together 1 cup sifted *powdered sugar* and enough *milk* (3 to 4 teaspoons) to make mixture of drizzling consistency.

157

Currant Swirl Loaf

You can buy pearl sugar in cake-decorating and Scandinavian shops, and by mail from companies specializing in baking supplies. Pictured opposite.

3½ to 4 cups all-purpose flour
  1 package active dry yeast
  1 cup milk
  ¼ cup margarine *or* butter
  3 tablespoons sugar
  ½ teaspoon salt
  2 eggs
  1 cup dried currants
  ½ cup water
  1 tablespoon lemon juice
  ⅓ cup packed brown sugar
  ½ teaspoon ground cinnamon
  2 tablespoons margarine *or* butter, melted
    Granulated sugar *or* pearl sugar

In a large mixer bowl combine *1½ cups* of the flour and yeast. In a small saucepan combine milk, the ¼ cup margarine, the 3 tablespoons sugar, and salt. Heat just till mixture is warm (115° to 120°) and margarine is almost melted, stirring constantly.

Add milk mixture and eggs to flour mixture. Beat with an electric mixer on low speed for 30 seconds, scraping sides of bowl. Beat on high speed for 3 minutes. Using a spoon, stir in as much of the remaining flour as you can.

Turn out onto a lightly floured surface. Knead in enough of the remaining flour to make a moder-

ately soft dough. Shape into a ball. Place in a lightly greased bowl, turning once to grease surface. Cover and let rise in a warm place till double (about 1 hour).

Meanwhile, in a saucepan combine the currants, water, and lemon juice. Bring to boiling. Let stand till cool. Drain, reserving liquid. Combine currants, brown sugar, and cinnamon. Set aside.

Punch dough down. Divide in half. Cover and let rest 10 minutes. On a floured surface roll one portion of dough into a 15x8-inch rectangle. Brush with some of the

reserved liquid. Sprinkle with *half* the currant mixture. Beginning at one narrow side, roll up jelly-roll style. Place in a greased 8x4x2-inch loaf pan. Repeat to make second loaf. Cover and let rise till nearly double (about 45 minutes).

Slit tops of loaves ½ inch deep (see photo, above). Carefully brush *each* with *half* of the melted margarine. Sprinkle with granulat-

ed sugar or pearl sugar. Bake in a 375° oven for 20 minutes. Cover with foil and bake 20 to 25 minutes longer or till done. Remove from pans to wire rack. Cool. Makes 2 loaves.

Whole Wheat-Carrot-Banana Bread

½ cup margarine *or* butter
  1 cup packed brown sugar
  2 eggs
  1 cup all-purpose flour
  1 cup whole wheat flour
  1 teaspoon baking soda
  ½ teaspoon baking powder
  ½ teaspoon salt
  ½ teaspoon ground cinnamon
  1 cup ripe mashed banana
  1 cup finely shredded carrot
  ½ cup chopped walnuts

In a mixer bowl beat margarine or butter for 30 seconds. Add sugar and beat fill fluffy. Beat in eggs. In a medium mixing bowl combine all-purpose flour, whole wheat flour, soda, baking powder, salt, and cinnamon. Add dry ingredients and banana alternately to sugar mixture, beating after each addition. Fold in carrots and nuts.

Pour into 2 greased 7½x3¾x2-inch loaf pans. Bake in a 350° oven for 40 to 50 minutes. Makes 2 loaves.

Overnight Breakfast Rolls

- 2 to 2½ cups all-purpose flour
- ¼ cup nonfat dry milk powder
- 1 package active dry yeast
- 1 egg
- ½ cup warm water (120° to 130°)
- ¼ cup shortening
- 2 tablespoons honey
- ¼ cup semisweet chocolate pieces
- ¼ cup peanut butter-flavored pieces
- 1 tablespoon margarine *or* butter
  Vanilla Glaze

Combine ¾ *cup* of the flour, dry milk, and yeast. Add egg, water, shortening, honey, and ¼ teaspoon *salt*. Beat at low speed of electric mixer for ½ minute. Beat 3 minutes at high speed. Stir in as much remaining flour as you can mix in using a spoon. Knead in enough remaining flour to make a moderately stiff dough that is smooth and elastic (6 to 8 minutes total). Shape into a ball. Place in a greased bowl, turning once. Cover; let rise in a warm place till double (about 1 hour). Punch dough down. Cover; let rest 10 minutes.

Meanwhile, melt chocolate pieces, peanut-butter-flavored pieces, and margarine. Cool slightly. Roll dough into a 12x8-inch rectangle. Spread chocolate mixture over dough. Roll up, jelly roll-style, beginning from longest side. Moisten edge with water; pinch to seal. Slice into 12 pieces. Place rolls in a greased 11x7x1½-inch baking pan. Cover loosely.

Refrigerate 2 to 24 hours.

Uncover rolls. Let stand at room temperature for 10 minutes. Break any surface bubbles using a greased wooden toothpick. Bake in a 375° oven for 20 to 25 minutes. Remove from pan. Drizzle with Vanilla Glaze. Makes 12.

Vanilla Glaze: Combine 1 cup sifted *powdered sugar,* ¼ teaspoon *vanilla,* and enough *milk* (1 to 2 tablespoons) to make of drizzling consistency.

Apricot Crescent Wreath

You'll find canned cake and pastry filling shelved with the other baking supplies in your supermaket. Don't substitute pie filling; it's not thick enough for this purpose.

- 1 package active dry yeast
- ¼ cup warm water (105° to 115°)
- 2 eggs
- 1 8-ounce carton dairy sour cream
- ¼ cup margarine *or* butter, melted
- ¼ cup sugar
- ½ teaspoon salt
- 2¾ to 3¼ cups all-purpose flour
- 1 12-ounce can apricot *or* cherry cake and pastry filling
- 1 cup sifted powdered sugar
- ½ cup flaked coconut

Soften yeast in warm water. In a large mixer bowl combine soft- ened yeast, eggs, sour cream, melted margarine, sugar, and salt. Beat till well combined.

Add 1½ *cups* of flour. Beat with electric mixer on low speed for 30 seconds, scraping bowl constantly. Beat at high speed for 3 minutes. Using a spoon, stir in as much of the remaining flour as you can.

Turn dough out onto a lightly floured surface. Knead in enough remaining flour to make a moder- ately soft dough that is smooth and elastic (3 to 5 minutes total). Place in a lightly greased bowl. Turn once to grease surface. Cov- er and let rise in a warm place till double (about 1½ hours).

Punch dough down. Divide in half. Shape each half into a ball. Cover and let rest for 10 minutes. Grease 2 baking sheets.

On a floured surface, roll half of the dough into a 12-inch circle. Spread with ⅓ cup (⅓ of the can) apricot or cherry filling. Cut into 12 wedges. Roll up wedges start- ing at wide end. On the greased baking sheet, arrange rolls in a cir- cle about ¼ inch apart. Repeat with remaining dough and ⅓ cup filling to make the second ring. Cover and let rise till almost dou- ble (about 30 minutes).

Bake in a 350° oven about 20 minutes or till done. Remove wreaths from baking sheets imme- diately. Cool on wire racks.

In a small bowl stir together powdered sugar, the remaining apricot or cherry filling, and enough *water* (about 2 table- spoons) to make the mixture of spreading consistency. Spread over the wreaths. Sprinkle each with coconut. Makes 2 wreaths, 12 servings each.

Christmastime

MEMORIES
1988

What Christmas Means to Me

Letters to Santa

Dear Santa,

_____

_____

_____

_____

_____

_____

_____

_____

_____

_____

_____

_____

_____

_____

_____

_____

_____

_____

_____

_____

_____

_____

_____

_____

_____

From:

Dear Santa,

From:

Letters to Santa

Dear Santa,

_____

_____

_____

_____

_____

_____

_____

_____

_____

_____

_____

_____

_____

_____

_____

_____

_____

_____

_____

_____

From:

Dear Santa,

From:

Color a Christmas Picture

Draw a Christmas Picture

Christmas Wish List

For family gift ideas

What _____ wants for Christmas _____

_____

_____

_____

What _____ wants for Christmas _____

_____

_____

_____

What _____ wants for Christmas _____

_____

_____

_____

What _____ wants for Christmas _____

_____

_____

_____

What _____ wants for Christmas _____

_____

_____

_____

Christmas Cards

Cards Sent _____
_____
_____
_____
_____
_____
_____
_____
_____
_____
_____
_____
_____
_____

Cards Received _____
_____
_____
_____
_____
_____
_____
_____
_____
_____
_____
_____
_____

Christmas Gifts

Gifts Given

_____

_____

_____

_____

_____

_____

_____

_____

_____

_____

_____

_____

_____

_____

_____

_____

_____

_____

_____

_____

_____

_____

_____

_____

Gifts Received

Holiday Get-Togethers

For remembering when we got together with family and friends

Where We Got Together _____

What We Did _____

_____

_____

_____

_____

_____

_____

_____

_____

_____

_____

Where We Got Together _____

What We Did _____

_____

_____

_____

_____

_____

_____

_____

_____

_____

_____

_____

Where We Got Together _____
What We Did _____
_____
_____
_____
_____
_____
_____
_____
_____
_____
_____
_____

Where We Got Together _____
What We Did _____
_____
_____
_____
_____
_____
_____
_____
_____
_____
_____
_____

Holiday Get-Togethers

For remembering when we got together with family and friends

Where We Got Together _____

What We Did _____

_____

_____

_____

_____

_____

_____

_____

_____

_____

_____

_____

_____

Where We Got Together _____

What We Did _____

_____

_____

_____

_____

_____

_____

_____

_____

_____

_____

_____

_____

_____

Where We Got Together _____
What We Did _____
_____
_____
_____
_____
_____
_____
_____
_____
_____

Where We Got Together _____
What We Did _____
_____
_____
_____
_____
_____
_____
_____
_____
_____
_____
_____

Holiday Favorites

Stories _____

_____

_____

_____

Carols _____

_____

_____

_____

Movies/TV Shows _____

_____

_____

_____

Poems _____

_____

_____

_____

Books _____

_____

_____

_____

Special Moments to Treasure

Photos and other holiday memorabilia

Special Moments to Treasure

Photos and other holiday memorabilia

Special Moments to Treasure

Photos and other holiday memorabilia

HOLIDAY DATEBOOK

1988
NOVEMBER

Thursday **24**	■ Thanksgiving Day (United States)
Friday **25**	
Saturday **26**	
Sunday **27**	
Monday **28**	
Tuesday **29**	
Wednesday **30**	

DECEMBER

Thursday **1**	
Friday **2**	
Saturday **3**	
Sunday **4**	

Monday
5

Tuesday
6

Wednesday
7

Thursday
8

Friday
9

Saturday
10

Sunday
11

Monday
12

Tuesday
13

Wednesday
14

Thursday
15

Friday
16

Saturday
17

Sunday
18

Monday **19**	
Tuesday **20**	
Wednesday **21**	
Thursday **22**	
Friday **23**	
Saturday **24**	■ Christmas Eve
Sunday **25**	■ Christmas Day
Monday **26**	■ Boxing Day (Canada)
Tuesday **27**	
Wednesday **28**	
Thursday **29**	
Friday **30**	
Saturday **31**	
Sunday **1**	■ New Year's Day

JANUARY

ACKNOWLEDGMENTS

Editor: Mary Helen Schiltz
Designer: Mary Schlueter Bendgen
Contributing Designer: Shelley Caldwell
Contributing Writers: Linda Henry, Debra Felton

We would like to express our gratitude and appreciation to the many people who granted us permission to use their stories, poems, illustrations, and photographs in our book:

Pages 2–3: Photograph by Neoma Thomas.

Pages 2–3: "Time for Christmas," reprinted with permission from THE GUIDEPOSTS CHRISTMAS TREASURY, Copyright © 1972 by Guideposts Associates, Inc., Carmel, New York.

Page 10: Illustration by J.C. Leyendecker. Reprinted from The Saturday Evening Post, Copyright © 1915, The Curtis Publishing Co.

Pages 11–12: "Jest 'fore Christmas," reprinted courtesy of The Scribner Book Company.

Pages 14–15: "Sliding," from WHISPERS AND OTHER POEMS by Myra Cohn Livingston, Copyright © 1958 by Myra Cohn Livingston. Reprinted by permission of Marian Reiner for the author.

Page 38: "A Real Santa Claus" reprinted courtesy of Houghton Mifflin Company.

Page 39: "Presents" reprinted from AROUND AND ABOUT, Copyright © 1957, renewed 1985. By permission of the author.

Pages 40–41: "An Alphabet of Christmas," reprinted with permission from Current, Inc., Colorado Springs, Colorado.

Page 48: Illustration by Norman Rockwell. Reprinted courtesy of Hallmark Cards Incorporated.

Page 49: "Hang Up the Baby's Stocking," Copyright © 1951 by Christian Herald Association, Inc. Used by permission.

Pages 50–51: "Golden Cobwebs," reprinted with permission of Kenneth Bennett, in behalf of author, Rowena Bastin Bennett.

Page 58: "A Gift for Mr. Guerney," reprinted with permission from Current, Inc., Colorado Springs, Colorado.

Page 59: Photograph by Robert Cushman Hayes.

Pages 66–67: Illustration by Currier & Ives. Courtesy of the Harry T. Peters Collection, Museum of the City of New York.

Pages 68–69: "Tommy's Letters," reprinted with permission of The Curtis Publishing Company.

Page 69: Illustration by Norman Rockwell. Reprinted courtesy of Hallmark Cards Incorporated.

Page 72: "On Going Home for Christmas," from COLLECTED VERSE by Edgar A. Guest, Copyright © 1934 by Contemporary Books, Inc. Reprinted by permission of Contemporary Books, Inc.

Page 87: "Ready for Christmas," reprinted from THE GUIDEPOSTS CHRISTMAS TREASURY, courtesy of Guideposts Associates, Inc., Carmel, New York.

Page 88: Photograph by Perry Struse, Rural American Graphics.

Page 89: "Grammy's Crèche," reprinted with permission from THE GUIDEPOSTS FAMILY CHRISTMAS BOOK, Copyright © 1980 by Guideposts Associates, Inc., Carmel, New York.

Page 90–91: Photograph by Perry Struse, Rural American Graphics.

Pages 92–94: "The Miraculous Staircase," reprinted with permission from GUIDEPOSTS magazine, Copyright © 1966 by Guideposts Associates, Inc., Carmel, New York.

Page 96: "A Tale for Christmas Evening," Copyright © 1951 by Christian Herald Association, Inc. Used by permission.

INDEX

STORIES

MEMORY PAGES

POEMS

CAROLS

Have BETTER HOMES AND
GARDENS® magazine
delivered to your door.
For information, write to:
MR. ROBERT AUSTIN
P.O. BOX 4536
DES MOINES, IA 50336